Liebe Schülerinnen und Schüler,

im folgenden Vokabelband findet ihr den **Basiswortschatz**, der für den **mittleren Bildungsabschluss** relevant ist.

Vital Vocabulary orientiert sich am gemeinsamen Europäischen Referenzrahmen für die **Niveaustufen A1 bis B1** und ist nach Themenbereichen geordnet.

Die englischen Wörter und ihre deutschen Entsprechungen befinden sich in den jeweiligen Tabellen.

In der Leiste am rechten Rand findet ihr Angaben zu **word families, synonyms, opposites** oder **irregular forms** (plurals, verbs). Hier ist meist auch noch Platz für eigene Notizen.

Bei den **word families** sind die Angaben in folgender Reihenfolge aufgelistet:

to accept   ·   *acceptance* · acceptable

↑   ↑   ↑

Verb (to-Infinitiv) - *Nomen (kursiv)* - Adjektiv

Nomen erkennt ihr hier also immer am *Kursivdruck*.

Auf jeder Seite befinden sich zudem **ausgewählte Beispielsätze** zu den Themengebieten.

Vital Vocabulary ist ein **Arbeitsband**, mit dessen Hilfe ihr bereits gelernte Wörter auffrischen und euch Vokabeln, die noch nicht bekannt sind, einprägen könnt. Sinnvoll ist es, unbekannte Wörter mit Leuchtstift zu markieren und sie regelmäßig zu wiederholen.

Gute Wortschatzarbeit ist die Grundlage für alle Speaking-, Listening-, Reading- und Writing-Aufgaben des mittleren Bildungsabschlusses. Sie stellt ebenso ein solides Fundament für alle dar, die auf dem Mittleren Abschluss aufbauen möchten.

Viel Erfolg wünscht euch

euer Team vom VOLL-Verlag

Inhaltsverzeichnis

Body and Health

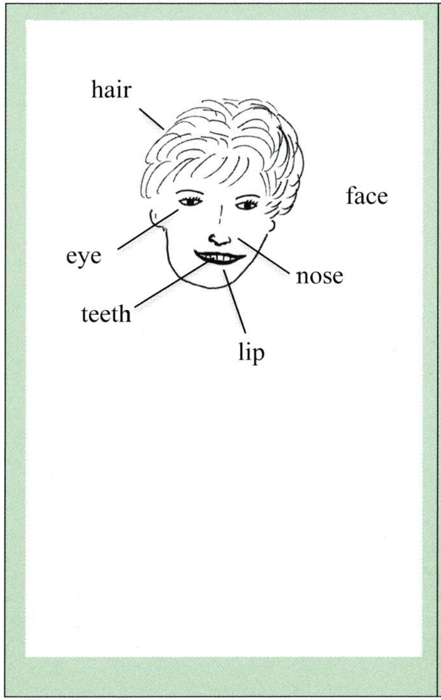

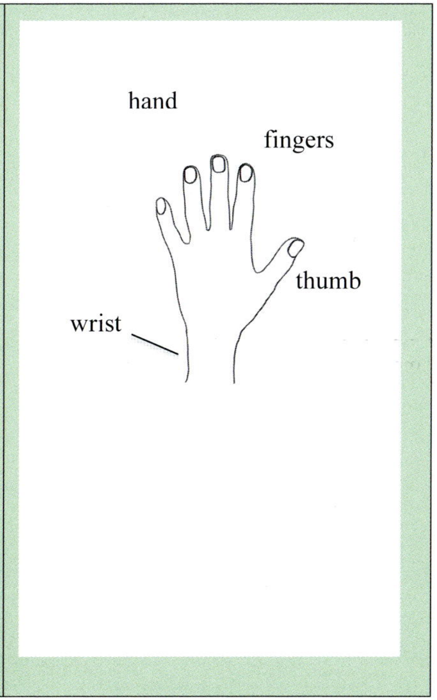

hair

face

eye

nose

teeth

lip

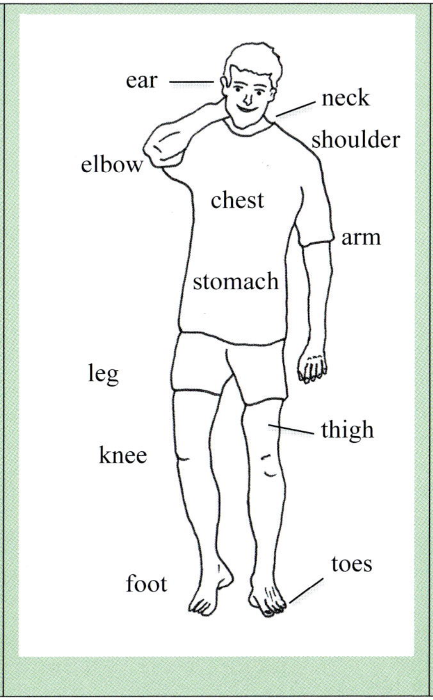

ear

neck

shoulder

elbow

chest

arm

stomach

leg

thigh

knee

foot

toes

hand

fingers

wrist

thumb

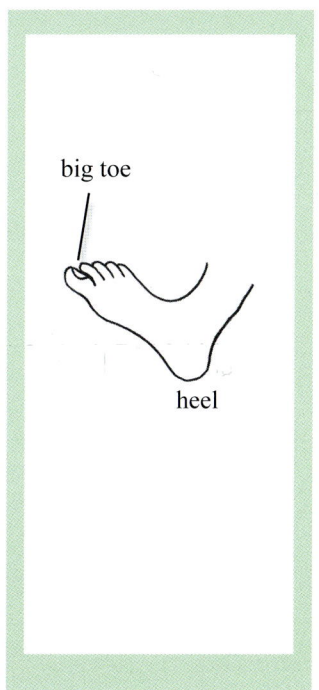

big toe

heel

1

Body and Health

body	Körper
head	Kopf
eye	Auge
to see	sehen
tear	Träne
to cry	weinen
nose	Nase
to smell	riechen
ear	Ohr
to hear	hören
to listen	zuhören
lip	Lippe
mouth	Mund
tooth	Zahn
to speak	sprechen
voice	Stimme
beard	Bart
face	Gesicht
freckles	Sommersprossen
hair	Haar, Haare

neck	Hals
throat	Kehle
shoulder	Schulter
muscle	Muskel
chest	Brust(-korb)
arm	Arm
heart	Herz
hand	Hand
finger	Finger
thumb	Daumen
elbow	Ellbogen
wrist	Handgelenk
fist	Faust
stomach	Magen, Bauch
belly	Bauch
leg	Bein
knee	Knie
heel	Ferse
toe	Zehe
foot	Fuß

thigh	Oberschenkel
nerve	Nerv
skin	Haut
figure	Figur, Körperbau
cell	Zelle
DNA	DNS
bone	Knochen
sense	Gespür, Gefühl
breath	Atem(-zug)
circulation	Kreislauf, Durchblutung
growth	Wachstum
memory	Gedächtnis
to sleep	schlafen
to yawn	gähnen
strength	Stärke, Kraft

word families:
to smell · *smell*
to speak · *speech*
to breathe · *breath* · breathless
to circulate · *circulation*
to grow · *growth*
to sleep · *sleep*
to strengthen · *strength* · strong

opposites:
to cry↔to laugh
to sleep↔to wake up
strength↔weakness

irregular verbs:
to see · saw · seen
to cry · cried · cried
to grow · grew · grown
to hear · heard · heard
to speak · spoke · spoken
to sleep · slept · slept

irregular plurals:
foot · feet
tooth · teeth

Beispielsätze: Annie cried when Arsenal lost the match. You could see the tears in her eyes. But Owen soon made her laugh again.

I don't feel well. I have a pain in my stomach (knee, shoulder, arm,…).

She has cute freckles on her nose. I think they make her look very young.

When you make a cake, it always smells lovely in the kitchen.

Body and Health

state	Zustand
healthy	gesund
bruised	mit blauen Flecken
ill	krank
fat	dick, fett
skinny	sehr dünn
overweight	übergewichtig
good-looking	gutaussehend
injured	verletzt
pale	bleich, blass
dizzy	schwindelig
sick	krank
sober	nüchtern
wrinkled	runzlig, faltig
absent-minded	zerstreut
awake	wach
alert	wach, munter
stiff	steif
to get a sunburn	Sonnenbrand bekommen

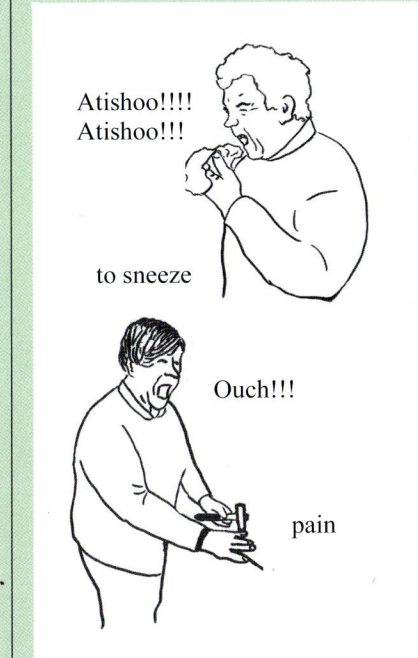

Atishoo!!!!
Atishoo!!!

to sneeze

Ouch!!!

pain

disorders / diseases	Krankheiten
headache	Kopfschmerzen
exhaustion	Erschöpfung
agony	Qual
pain	Schmerz
fever	Fieber
shock	Schock
coma	Koma
to collapse	zusammenbrechen
to faint	ohnmächtig werden
to hurt	weh tun
emergency	Notfall
to shiver	zittern
to sneeze	niesen
cancer	Krebs
diarrhoea	Durchfall
malaria	Malaria
smallpox	Pocken
flu	Grippe

word families:
to heal · *health* · healthy
to bruise · *bruise* · bruised
illness · ill
to weigh · *weight* ·
overweight
to injure · *injury* · injured
to wrinkle · *wrinkle* ·
wrinkled
sunburn · sunburnt
to shiver · *shiver* · shivering

opposites:
healthy↔unhealthy, ill, sick
fat↔thin
overweight↔underweight
sober↔drunk
stiff↔relaxed
absent-minded↔alert
awake↔sleepy

irregular verbs:
to hurt · hurt · hurt

Beispielsätze: Eating vegetables is very healthy. It prevents illness, a lot of experts say.

Miranda says she feels dizzy. She looks pale, too. I hope she is not going to faint. Maybe she is ill. She should see a doctor, I think.

It's hard to concentrate when you have a headache or some other form of pain.

Body and Health

treatment	Behandlung
medicine	Medizin
bandage	Verband
to vaccinate	impfen
to rescue	retten, bergen
surgery	Arztpraxis, Behandlungsraum, Chirurgie, Operation
waiting room	Wartezimmer
ambulance	Krankenwagen
hospital	Krankenhaus
to X-ray	röntgen
to recover	sich erholen
diet	Diät
to examine	untersuchen

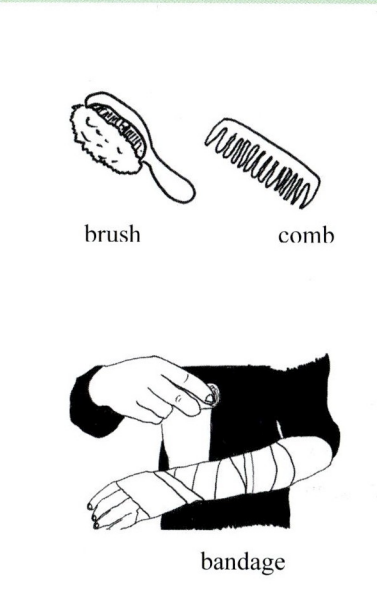

brush   comb

bandage

life	Leben
corpse	Leiche
survival	Überleben
to be born	geboren werden
to exist	existieren
death	Tod
to die	sterben
cosmetics	Kosmetika
to wash	waschen
to brush	bürsten
to comb	kämmen
to bathe	baden
soap	Seife
mirror	Spiegel
to look at	anschauen
to stare	starren

word families:
to vaccinate · *vaccination*
to rescue · *rescue*
to recover · *recovery*
to examine · *examination*
to live · *life* · *lively*
to survive · *survival*
to exist · *existence*
to die · *death*
to bathe · *bath*

irregular verbs:
to die · died · died

irregular plurals:
life · lives

Beispielsätze: Were you vaccinated against hepatitis when you went on holiday to India?

The ambulance took the injured man to hospital. There he was thoroughly examined and X-rayed. Nothing was broken. He is already recovering from his injuries.

She looked at herself in the mirror, combed and brushed her long hair, and put her make-up on.

Body and Health

to sit	sitzen
to stand	stehen
to imagine	sich vorstellen
to think	denken
to worry	sich Sorgen machen
to smell	riechen
to touch	berühren
to miss	vermissen, fehlen
to stretch	dehnen
to fall	fallen
to look forward to	sich freuen auf
to step	treten, schreiten
to walk	gehen
to move	sich bewegen
to run	rennen
to go	gehen

to whisper

to smell

to be	sein
to care for	betreuen, sich kümmern um
to care about	Zuneigung empfinden, wichtig nehmen
to take care of	sich kümmern um
to say	sagen
to whisper	flüstern
to shout	schreien
to yell	brüllen
to scream	schreien
to sigh	seufzen

fresh	frisch
hard	hart, schwierig
confident	selbstsicher, zuversichtlich
essential	wesentlich, wichtig

word families:
to imagine · *imagination*
to think · *thought*
to worry · *worry* · worried
to smell · *smell* · smelly
to miss · *missing*
to move · *move* · moving
to care · *care* · caring
to scream · *scream* · screaming
confidence · confident
essence · essential

opposites:
death↔life
to die↔to live

irregular verbs:
to sit · sat · sat
to stand · stood · stood
to think · thought · thought
to fall · fell · fallen
to run · ran · run
to go · went · gone
to be · was · been
to say · said · said

Beispielsätze:
Imagine winning the lottery! That would be really great!
Well, I don't miss anything and am quite happy as long as I stay healthy and fit.
It is very important to move, do sports, eat healthy food, and take care of your body.
I really look forward to running a marathon next year.

Clothes

items of clothing	Kleidungsstücke
pullover	Pullover
sweater	Pullover
sweatshirt	Sweatshirt
cardigan	Strickjacke
jacket	Jacke
coat	Mantel
scarf	Schal
suit	Anzug, Kostüm
skirt	Rock
dress	Kleid
blouse	Bluse
shirt	Hemd
tie	Krawatte
trousers	Hose
shorts	kurze Hose
tights	Strumpfhose
sock	Socke

device garb · Gerät · Gewand

dressing gown	Bademantel
nightdress	Nachthemd
pyjamas	Schlafanzug
tracksuit	Trainingsanzug
anorak	Windjacke
shoes	Schuhe
trainers	Sportschuhe
boot, boots	Stiefel
to try on	anprobieren
to fit	passen

material	Material
cotton	Baumwolle
denim	Jeansstoff
silk	Seide
linen	Leinen
wool	Wolle

accessories	modisches Zubehör
handbag	Handtasche
handkerchief	Taschentuch
jewellery	Schmuck
bracelet	Armband
ring	Ring
umbrella	Regenschirm

style	Stil
fashionable	modisch, schick
old-fashioned	altmodisch
modern	modern

details	einzelne Elemente
hood	Kapuze
zipper	Reißverschluss
pocket	Tasche
sleeve	Ärmel

word families:
fashion· fashionable· old-fashioned

irregular verbs:
to try on· tried on· tried on
to fit· fit· fit

plurals without singular forms:
trousers
shorts
tights
pyjamas
jeans
glasses

irregular plurals:
scarf· scarves

scarf

shirt
tie

Beispielsätze:
You should put on a jacket. It is quite cold today.
These jeans look fantastic. Can I try them on?
What size are those shoes?
Mummy, can you tie my shoelaces?
Where **are** my pyjamas (trousers/ jeans/ glasses/ tights)?
These trainers fit quite well.

zipper

cardigan

sleeve

Food and Drinks / In the Kitchen

fruit	Frucht, Früchte
apple	Apfel
banana	Banane
grape	Traube
pineapple	Ananas
cherry	Kirsche
peach	Pfirsich
pear	Birne

drinks	Getränke
tea	Tee
coffee	Kaffee
juice	Saft
water	Wasser
milk	Milch
lemonade	Limonade
wine	Wein
beer	Bier

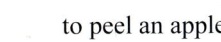

to peel an apple

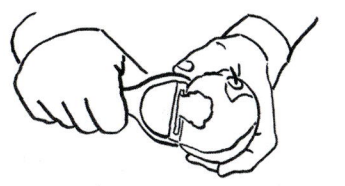

vegetables	Gemüse
bean	Bohne
cabbage	Kohl
carrot	Karotte
tomato	Tomate
mushroom	Pilz
pumpkin	Kürbis
courgette	Zucchini
potato	Kartoffel

meat	Fleisch
beef	Rindfleisch
pork	Schweinefleisch
lamb	Lammfleisch
veal	Kalbfleisch
turkey	Truthahn
chicken	Huhn, Hähnchen
mutton	Schaffleisch, Hammelfleisch
sausage	Wurst
bacon	Speck
ham	Schinken
burger	Frikadelle
mince	Hackfleisch

fish and seafood	Fisch und Meeresfrüchte
lobster	Hummer
trout	Forelle
prawns	Krabben
mussels	Muscheln

irregular plurals:
tomato · tomatoes
potato · potatoes

Beispielsätze: Eating lots of vegetables is very healthy.
Vegetarians don't eat meat.
I like most of vegetables, but I can't stand cabbage.
I am thirsty. Could I have some mineral water, please?

Food and Drinks / In the Kitchen

more food	weitere Lebensmittel
bread	Brot
toast	Toast
butter	Butter
cream	Sahne
cheese	Käse
cereal	Getreideflocken
muesli	Müsli
rice	Reis
egg	Ei
honey	Honig
jam	Marmelade
flour	Mehl
wheat	Weizen

a slice of bread	eine Scheibe Brot
a loaf of bread	ein Laib Brot

at the restaurant	im Restaurant
waiter	Ober, Kellner
waitress	Kellnerin, Bedienung
to tip	Trinkgeld geben
tip	Trinkgeld
menu	Speisekarte
starter	Vorspeise
main course	Hauptspeise
dessert	Nachspeise
tablecloth	Tischtuch
napkin	Serviette
to order	bestellen
to pay	bezahlen

snacks and sweets	Zwischenmahl-zeiten und Süßigkeiten
sandwich	belegtes Brötchen
biscuit	Keks
cake	Kuchen
cookie	Keks
nuts	Nüsse
chocolate	Schokolade
chewing gum	Kaugummi
ice-cream	Speiseeis
snack	Zwischenmahlzeit
crisps	Kartoffelchips
popcorn	Popcorn

word families:
to tip · *tip*
to order · *order*

irregular plurals:
loaf · loaves

waiter

MENU

Beispielsätze: Could we have the bill, please?
You usually tip a waiter or waitress at the restaurant.

Could you pass me the menu, please? I'd like to have a dessert.
What are you having?
I think I may order chocolate cake.

Food and Drinks / In the Kitchen

dishes	Gerichte
soup	Suppe
pie	Pastete
chips (B.E.)	Pommes Frites
French Fries (A.E)	Pommes Frites
pasta	Nudeln
pizza	Pizza
sauce	Soße
curry	Currygericht
porridge	Haferbrei
salad	Salat
pancake	Pfannkuchen
baked beans	Bohnen in Tomatensoße

tastes	Geschmacksrichtungen
to taste	schmecken
sweet	süß
sour	sauer
hot	scharf
salty	salzig
bitter	bitter

sour

hot

sweet

cooking	kochen
to cook	kochen
to boil	kochen, sieden
to fry	braten
to peel	schälen
to stir	rühren, umrühren
to prepare	vorbereiten
recipe	Rezept

to stir

spices	Gewürze
salt	Salz
pepper	Pfeffer
cloves	Nelken
sugar	Zucker

word families:
to taste · *taste* · tasty
to cook · *cooking* · cooked
to boil · boiled
to fry · fried
to peel · *peel* · peeled
to stir · stirred
to prepare · *preparation* · prepared

opposites:
sweet↔sour

Beispielsätze: In Britain a lot of takeaways offer fish and chips.
Bernhard says the chips there taste far better than the ones we get over here.

Could I have the recipe for the fried vegetables?

(...) Add the carrots and fry them for 3-4 minutes. Stir in the other ingredients and cook for another three minutes before serving.

9

Food and Drinks / In the Kitchen

in the kitchen	in der Küche
plate	Teller
knife	Messer
spoon	Löffel
fork	Gabel
glass	Glas
teaspoon	Teelöffel
cup	Tasse
bowl	Schüssel
frying pan	Bratpfanne
cooker	Herd
tray	Tablett
saucepan	Topf

frying pan

cooker

bowl

meals	Mahlzeiten
breakfast	Frühstück
lunch	Mittagessen
tea	leichte Mahlzeit am Spätnachmittag
dinner	Abendessen
supper	leichte Mahlzeit am Abend
picnic	Picknick
barbecue	Grillfeier

teaspoon

fork

spoon

plate knife

irregular plurals:
knife · knives

Beispielsätze: May I invite you for dinner tonight?

We had a barbecue with friends at the weekend.
The weather was fantastic and we really enjoyed eating outside.

Shopping

shop	Geschäft
store (AE)	Geschäft, Laden
bookshop	Buchhandlung
newsagent's	Zeitungshändler
chemist's	Apotheke, Drogerie
bakery	Bäckerei
butcher's shop	Metzgerei
supermarket	Supermarkt
pet shop	Zoogeschäft

assistant	Verkäufer/in
customer	Kunde/Kundin
cashier	Kassierer/in

to buy	kaufen
to sell	verkaufen
to advertise	Werbung machen (für)
on sale	zu verkaufen
sale, sales	Schlussverkauf
cheap	billig
storage	Lagerung
goods	Waren
receipt	Quittung
voucher	Gutschein
bag	Tasche
escalator	Rolltreppe

escalator

buildings and sections	Gebäude und Abteilungen
café	Café
cafeteria	Cafeteria
to have a cup of coffee	eine Tasse Kaffee trinken
shopping centre (B.E.)	Einkaufszentrum
shopping mall (A.E.)	Einkaufszentrum
warehouse	Lagerhalle
cash desk	Kasse
counter	Theke
department store	Warenhaus
market	Markt
stall	Stand (auf dem Markt)
to offer	anbieten
to compare	vergleichen
bill	Rechnung

word families:
to advertise · *advertisement* · *ad*
to sell · *sale* · sold
to store · *storage* · stored

opposites:
cheap↔expensive
to buy↔to sell

irregular verbs:
to buy · bought · bought
to sell · sold · sold

Beispielsätze:
You can buy meat at the butcher's or at the supermarket.
Can you get me a newspaper at the newsagent's, please?
We still have to get some cat food at the pet shop.
There is a long queue at the check out.
The assistant asked me if I would like to have a receipt.
I think we will get Elena a gift voucher for her birthday.

People and Family

family and tradition	Familie und Tradition
parents	Eltern
mother	Mutter
father	Vater
daughter	Tochter
son	Sohn
grandfather	Großvater
grandmother	Großmutter
child	Kind
grandchild	Enkel(-kind)

man	Mann
woman	Frau
girl	Mädchen
boy	Junge

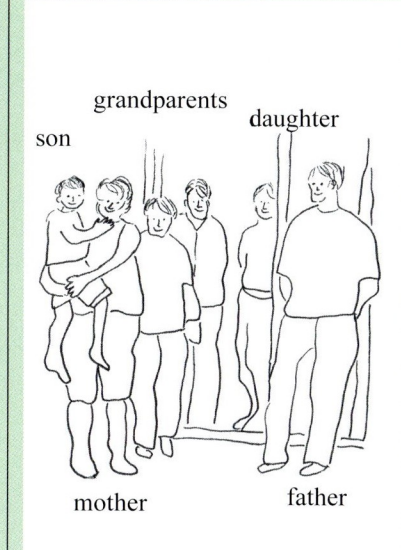

cousin	Cousin/e
uncle	Onkel
aunt	Tante
relative	Verwandte/r
nephew	Neffe
niece	Nichte
husband	Ehemann
wife	Ehefrau
sister	Schwester
brother	Bruder
in-laws	angeheiratete Verwandte

word families:
to relate · *relative* · *relationship* · related

irregular plurals:
child · children
wife · wives
man · men
woman · women

Beispielsätze: I have relatives in the US. My mother's sister lives there.
She has three children: one son and two daughters.
So far, I have never met my aunt and cousins, but I am planning to visit them next spring.
My sister-in-law will come with me.

People and Family

characteristics	Eigenschaften
careless	nachlässig
careful	vorsichtig
disciplined	diszipliniert
faithful	treu, getreu
kind	freundlich, nett
nice	nett, schön
ordinary	gewöhnlich, normal
patient	geduldig
shy	schüchtern
confident	selbstbewusst
courageous	mutig
sensible	vernünftig
sensitive	einfühlsam, empfindlich

"Be careful!
The floor is wet,
here!"

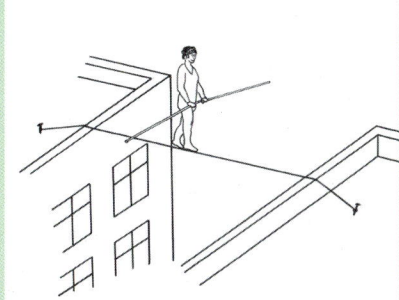

You have to be quite
courageous, careful and
disciplined to do this.

reliable	zuverlässig
clever	klug, schlau
crazy	verrückt
friendly	freundlich
funny	lustig, seltsam
intelligent	intelligent
beautiful	schön
stupid	blöd, dumm
lazy	faul
rude	unhöflich, grob
jealous	eifersüchtig
nasty	gemein, fies, böse, übel
generous	großzügig
polite	höflich
strange	seltsam
silly	dumm, albern

lazy

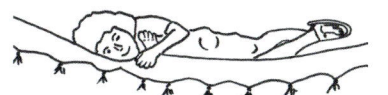

word families:
to care · *care* · careless · caring
to have faith in · faithful
kindness · kind
patience · patient
to encourage s.o. · *courage* · courageous
to rely on s.o. · reliable
intelligence · intelligent
beauty · beautiful
stupidity · stupid
laziness · lazy
generosity · generous
politeness · polite

opposites:
careless↔careful
faithful↔untrue, unfaithful
kind↔unkind
ordinary↔special
patient↔impatient
shy↔confident
reliable↔unreliable
clever↔stupid
intelligent↔stupid
beautiful↔ugly
rude↔nice, polite
polite↔impolite

synonyms:
ordinary ≈ normal
courageous ≈ brave
clever ≈ intelligent

Beispielsätze: I can't understand how you can be so patient. It drives me crazy to stand in a queue for hours.
Cindy's new boyfriend is very jealous. He doesn't want her to go out on her own.
It is easy to like someone who is always kind, polite and generous.

People and Family

feelings	Gefühle
love	Liebe
hate	Hass
shame	Schande, Scham
confusion	Verwirrung
excitement	Aufregung
fear	Angst, Furcht
fright	Angst, Furcht
panic	Panik
hope	Hoffnung
pride	Stolz
happiness	Glück, Freude, Glücksgefühl
sadness	Traurigkeit

to look after	sich kümmern um
to comfort	trösten
to look	aussehen, sehen
to enjoy	genießen
to change	wechseln, sich verändern
to cry	weinen, schreien
to laugh	lachen
to grow up	(auf-)wachsen
to obey	gehorchen
to fool	zum Narren halten
to shut up	den Mund halten
to tease s.o.	jmd. aufziehen, ärgern, necken
to hang out	herumhängen
to help	helfen
to imagine	sich vorstellen
to dream	träumen
to please	gefallen
to like	mögen

honour	Ehre
to be honoured	geehrt sein
somebody	jemand
someone	jemand
nobody	niemand
no one	niemand

to obey

word families:
to confuse · *confusion* · confused
to excite · *excitement* · excited
to frighten s.o. · *fright* · frightened
to hope · *hope* · hopeful · hopeless
pride · proud
to comfort · *comfort*
to enjoy · *enjoyment* · enjoyable

opposites:
love↔hate
confusion↔clarity
fear↔confidence
happiness↔sadness
to cry↔to laugh
to like↔to dislike
somebody↔nobody
someone↔no one

synonyms:
to look after ≈ to care for

irregular verbs:
to cry · cried · cried
to grow (up) · grew · grown
to shut (up) · shut · shut
to hang (out) · hung · hung
to dream · dreamt · dreamt

Beispielsätze: There has been a lot of confusion in our company. A new investor has taken it over.
The fear of losing their jobs and being unemployed troubles a lot of employees.
Things don't look too good, I'd say.
A lot of people are trying to get a job somewhere else because they fear the company might be completely closed down.
Although I have always liked it here, I will try to change jobs, too.

People and Family

relationship	Beziehung
marriage	Ehe, Heirat
to get along with	auskommen mit, sich gut verstehen mit
to get on with	auskommen mit
girlfriend	(feste) Freundin
boyfriend	(fester) Freund
harmony	Harmonie
couple	Paar
difference	Unterschied
to disagree	nicht übereinstimmen
to divorce s.o.	sich von jemandem scheiden lassen
to separate	sich trennen
to discuss	besprechen, diskutieren
partner	Partner/in
engagement	Verlobung

"It's about time that Fred and I got a divorce."

"I disagree with you. You should both try to save your marriage."

typical of s.o. or s.th.	typisch für jemanden oder etwas
ugly	hässlich
to be unable to do s.th.	unfähig sein, etwas zu tun
weak	schwach
strong	stark
young	jung
normal	normal
personal	persönlich
rough	rau, grob
smart	geschickt, schlau
usually	gewöhnlich
to surprise s.o.	jemanden überraschen
to swear	fluchen, schwören

word families:
to marry · to get married · *marriage* · married
to differ · *difference* · different
to disagree · *disagreement*
to divorce s.o. · *divorce*
to separate · *separation*
to discuss · *discussion*
to get engaged · *engagement*

opposites:
harmony↔conflict
difference↔similarity
to agree↔to disagree
to separate↔to unite
ugly↔beautiful
able↔unable
weak↔strong
young↔old
normal↔abnormal
smart↔stupid

synonyms:
smart ≈ intelligent
usually ≈ normally

irregular verbs
to swear · swore · sworn

Beispielsätze: It is not always easy to have a good relationship with your partner.
Unfortunately, more and more couples separate and divorce.
A couple who has been happily married for 30 years said:
"A happy marriage is the union of two good forgivers.
We have always managed to get along with each other and leave each other space.
Of course, we have also disagreed and had our arguments, but we have always managed to find peace and harmony again."

People and Family

to leave	weggehen, verlassen
to mean	bedeuten
to let	lassen
to meet	treffen
to promise	versprechen
to recognize	erkennen, begreifen
to refuse	sich weigern
to remind s.o. of s.th.	jemanden an etwas erinnern
to rest	ausruhen
to return	zurückkehren
to search	suchen
to regard	betrachten
to remain	bleiben
to welcome	begrüßen, empfangen
to come	kommen
to greet	grüßen

"I would like to become a doctor when I grow up."

present	Geschenk
to become	werden
to have	haben
to hold	halten
mustn't	nicht dürfen
to need	brauchen
to pretend	vortäuschen
to take	nehmen
to visit	besuchen
to want	wollen
to lean	(sich) lehnen, (sich) beugen

Beispielsätze: "Mum, please, can I go out tonight? I promise I will be back on time."
"What time do you think you will return home? You know you were late last Sunday. I was very worried and almost got into the car to search for you."
"I'll take the bus at ten, so I should be here at quarter past ten."
"Alright, but don't drink any alcohol, please."

School

worksheets	Arbeitsblätter
bracket	Klammer
capital letter	Großbuchstabe
to colour	färben, anmalen
false / wrong	falsch
right /true	richtig
correct	richtig
to hand in	abgeben
to hand out	austeilen
odd one out	nicht dazugehörig
underlined	unterstrichen
to collect	(ein-)sammeln
to compare	vergleichen
to complete	vervollständigen
to draw	zeichnen
example	Beispiel
exercise	Übung, Aufgabe

grid	Tabelle
heading	Überschrift
italics	Kursivschrift
line	Linie, Zeile
synonym	Synonym (Wort mit gleicher Bedeutung)
opposite	Gegenteil
page	Seite
question mark	Fragezeichen
exclamation mark	Ausrufezeichen
comma	Komma
dot, full stop	Punkt
hyphen	Bindestrich
quotation mark	Anführungs-zeichen

? question mark **-** hyphen

life at school	Schulleben
to be missing	fehlen
assembly	Versammlung
excursion	Ausflug
lesson / period	Unterrichtsstunde
to bully	tyrannisieren
locker	Schließfach
pupil (B.E.)	Schüler/in
student (A.E.)	Schüler/in,
class, form (B.E.)	Klasse
grade (A.E.)	Klasse
detention	Nachsitzen
school exchange	Schüleraustausch
to mix up	vermischen

"   "   quotation marks

word families:
to correct · *correction*
to collect · *collection*
to compare · *comparison*
to complete · *completion* · complete
to draw · *drawing*
to bully s.o. · *bully* · *bullying* · bullied

opposites:
true↔false
right↔wrong
correct↔incorrect
to hand in↔to hand out

prepositions:
to hand in
to hand out
to compare to
to mix up

Beispielsätze:
Complete the worksheets.
Put the words in brackets into their correct form.
The months in English are spelled with a capital letter.
Find the odd one out.
Replace the underlined words with a word from the same word family.
Find a suitable heading.
Who is missing today?
Assembly is at half past eight every morning.
Pupils who often forget their homework are given a detention in the lunch break.

School

subjects	Fächer; Themen
maths	Mathematik
science	Naturwissen-schaft (-en)
physics	Physik
chemistry	Chemie
biology	Biologie
English	Englisch
German	Deutsch
French	Französisch
geography	Erdkunde
art	Kunst
music	Musik
history	Geschichte
physical education (P.E.)	Sport
home economics, domestic science	Hauswirtschaft
religious education (R.E.)	Religionsunter-richt

lessons	Unterrichtsstun-den
to repeat	wiederholen
to listen	zuhören
to read	lesen
to write	schreiben
to spell	buchstabieren
to sum up	zusammenfassen
to summarize	zusammenfassen
to retell	nacherzählen
topic	Thema
to concentrate on	sich konzentrieren auf
to take turns	sich abwechseln
unit	Lektion, Kapitel
to define	definieren
to explain	erklären
to express	ausdrücken
to forget	vergessen

gist	das Wichtigste
complicated	kompliziert
to describe	beschreiben
to distract	ablenken
handwriting	Handschrift
to interrupt	unterbrechen
to know	wissen, kennen
to notice	bemerken, sehen
to paraphrase	umschreiben

building	Gebäude
classroom	Klassenzimmer
assembly hall	Aula
corridor	Flur
gym	Turnhalle
playground	Pausenhof, Spielplatz
office	Büro

word families:
to write · *writer*
to summarize · *summary*
to concentrate · *concentration*
to define · *definition*
to explain · *explanation*
to express · *expression*
complication · complicated
to describe · *description*
to distract · *distraction*
to interrupt · *interruption*
to know · *knowledge*

synonyms:
to notice ≈ to see

opposites:
to remember↔to forget
complicated↔easy

irregular verbs:
to read · read · read
to write · wrote · written
to retell · retold · retold
to take (turns) · took · taken
to forget · forgot · forgotten
to know · knew · known

Beispielsätze:
Could you repeat what you have just said? I didn't get it.
Could you spell your name, please?
Summarize the text.
Please, concentrate on the topic.
We always take turns cleaning the board.
Try to get the gist of the text.
Our teacher doesn't like being interrupted.
Paraphrase the underlined words, please.

School

studying and learning	Studieren und Lernen
basics	Grundwissen
to begin	anfangen
break	Pause
to attend	besuchen
essay	Aufsatz
to practise	üben
foreign language	Fremdsprache
fluent	fließend
to pronounce	aussprechen
to translate	übersetzen
homework	Hausaufgaben
to improve	verbessern
method	Methode
to understand	verstehen

exams	Prüfungen
GCSE	Prüfung ab 15 in Großbritannien
to graduate	einen Schulabschluss machen
high school diploma (A.E.)	Abschluss der High School
school leaver	Schulabgänger/in
to prepare for	sich vorbereiten (auf)
to register	sich einschreiben
certificate	Zeugnis
grade, mark	Note
mistake	Fehler
grammar	Grammatik

staff	Personal
head teacher	Schuldirektor/in
principal (A.E.)	Schuldirektor/in
professor	Professor/in
teacher	Lehrer/in
secretary	Sekretär/in

high school graduation

diploma

word families:
to begin · *beginning* · *beginner*
to practise · *practice*
fluency · fluent
to pronounce · *pronunciation*
to translate · *translation*
to improve · *improvement*
to graduate · *graduate* · *graduation*
to prepare · *preparation*
to register · *register*

synonyms:
to begin ≈ to start

opposites:
to begin ↔ to end

Beispielsätze:
You need to know the basics in maths to pass the test.
Linda is very good at writing essays.
Can you speak a foreign language?
Yes, I am fluent in French.
The GCSE-results are important for your further career.
For certain subjects like medicine and law you need to have good grades.

School

material and equipment	Material und Ausrüstung
biro	Kugelschreiber
paper	Papier
sheet	Blatt
fountain pen	Füller
pencil	Bleistift
to sharpen	spitzen
blackboard	Schultafel
rubber	Radiergummi
ruler	Lineal
crayon	Buntstift
dictionary	Wörterbuch
desk	Pult, Schreibtisch
folder	Mappe, Hefter
poster	Plakat
transparency	Folie
exercise book	Übungsheft
school uniform	Schuluniform

types of schools	Schularten
nursery school	Kindergarten
primary school (B.E.), elementary school (A.E.)	Grundschule
secondary school	weiterführende Schule
comprehensive school (B.E.)	Gesamtschule

junior school (A.E.)	Schule für die Mittelstufe
high school (A.E.)	Schule für die Oberstufe

boarding school	Internat
college	Hochschule
university	Universität

especially	besonders
certain	sicher
easy	leicht
to succeed in	Erfolg haben mit
to find	finden
to guess	raten, erraten
to remark	eine Bemerkung machen
to remember	sich erinnern
simple	einfach
to study	lernen, untersuchen
to inspire	anregen, begeistern
must	müssen
to pass	reichen, bestehen
to receive	erhalten
to interfere	sich einmischen, eingreifen

Beispielsätze:
May I sharpen the pencil, please?
Open your exercise books, please.
Pupils who go to a boarding school get meals at school and live there during the school term.
Remember to bring tennis shoes with you tomorrow.
Susan passed her test in maths. She was delighted.
Could you pass me your book, please?

Games

board game	Brettspiel
chess	Schach
rule	Regel
dice (pl)	Würfel
lottery	Lotterie
luck	Glück
to be lucky	Glück haben
aim	Ziel
balloon	Luftballon
to bet	wetten
ribbon	Band
to spoil a game	ein Spiel verderben
to cheat	betrügen, mogeln

leisure	Freizeit
recreation	Entspannung, Erholung
to relax	(sich) entspannen
winner	Gewinner/in
loser	Verlierer/in

to play	spielen
to gamble	um Geld spielen
unlimited	unbegrenzt
to be unlucky	Pech haben
fortunately	glücklicherweise
to take part in	teilnehmen an
to take place	stattfinden

chess

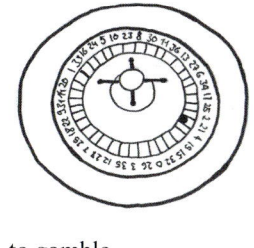

to gamble

Beispielsätze:
It is never too late to learn how to play chess.
The aim is to capture or trap your opponent's king.
You should always try to think a few moves ahead.

A woman in Wexford was lucky. She won the lottery on Saturday. She said she just wanted to go on a holiday with the money and relax.
It was the first time she had taken part. She usually doesn't gamble at all.

Sports

athletics	Leichtathletik
athlete	Sportler/in
fitness	Fitness, Kondition
to throw	werfen
sprint	Sprint
to jump	springen
competitor	Konkurrent/in, Teilnehmer/in
effort	Anstrengung
kit	Ausrüstung
league	Bündnis, Liga
enthusiasm	Begeisterung
fantastic	fantastisch
sponsor	Sponsor
instructor	Ausbilder/in
trainer	Trainer/in
close	knapp, nahe
to compete	im Wettbewerb stehen, gegeneinander antreten

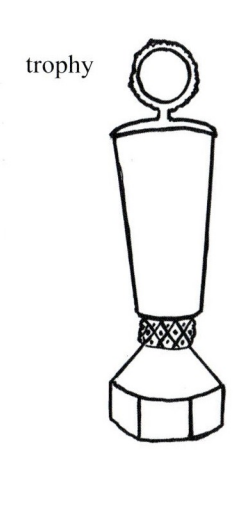

trophy

opponent	Gegner/in
challenge	Herausforderung
chance	Möglichkeit
crowd	Menschenmenge
supporter	Anhänger/in
to cheer	zujubeln, anfeuern
mascot	Maskottchen
to congratulate on	gratulieren zu
award	Auszeichnung, Preis
trophy	Pokal
to fall over	hinfallen
to finish	beenden, ins Ziel kommen
to get ready	sich vorbereiten
to give up	aufgeben
to go ahead	vorangehen
to join	sich anschließen, beitreten

word families:
athlete · athletics · athletic
to compete · *competitor*
competition · competitive
enthusiasm · enthusiastic
to sponsor · *sponsor ·*
sponsorship
to instruct · *instruction ·*
instructive
to train · *trainer · training ·*
trained
to challenge · *challenge*
to support · *supporter*
to cheer · *cheerleader*
to congratulate ·
congratulation
to award · *award ·* awarding

synonyms:
fantastic ≈ wonderful, brilliant
to attempt ≈ to try
kit ≈ equipment
chance ≈ opportunity
supporter ≈ fan
to finish ≈ to end, to complete

irregular verbs:
to throw · threw · thrown
to fall (over) · fell · fallen
to get (ready) · got · got
to give (up) · gave · given
to go (ahead) · went · gone

Beispielsätze: Every four years athletes from all over the world compete at the Olympic Games and enjoy the challenge.

During a marathon a runner fell close to the finish line. Other runners helped him over the line and the crowd cheered.
On completing the marathon, he was congratulated for not giving up.

Sports

football (B.E.)	Fußball
soccer (A.E.)	Fußball
pitch	Spielfeld
player	Spieler/in
referee	Schiedsrichter/in
to whistle	pfeifen
goal	Tor
goalkeeper	Torwart
to kick	treten
stadium	Stadion
final	Finale, Endspiel
foul	Foul
to score	ein Tor erzielen
to tackle	angreifen

tennis	Tennis
racket	Schläger
ball	Ball
net	Netz

cycling	Fahrradfahren
helmet	Helm
handlebars (pl)	Lenkstange
bicycle, bike	Fahrrad
to ride a bike	Rad fahren
to cycle	Rad fahren
skiing	Skifahren
to ski	Ski fahren
canoeing	Kanufahren
canoe	Kanu
to paddle	paddeln
archery	Bogenschießen
bow	Bogen
arrow	Pfeil
hunting	Jagen
binoculars	Fernglas

a football pitch

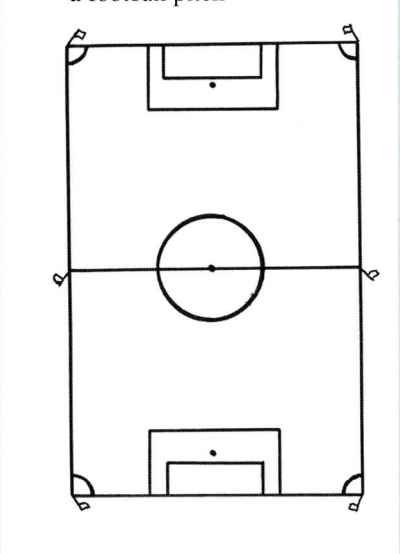

word families:
to play · *player*
to whistle · *whistle*
final · finally · final
to score · *score*
to paddle · *paddle*
to hunt · *hunter* · *hunting*

synonyms:
to ride a bike ≈ to cycle

Beispielsätze:

Being a referee is a very demanding job.
You have to run more than the players and must make decisions about goals, foul play, red or yellow cards, and penalties. If you make a mistake, a lot of people will be cross.

Cyclists should always wear a helmet to avoid head injuries. Even at the speed that cyclists reach, the damage can be fatal.

Binoculars are very useful for watching the deer while hunting.

Sports

cricket	engl. Rasensport
rugby	Rugby
basketball	Basketball
volleyball	Volleyball
badminton	Federballspiel
baseball	Baseball
fencing	Fechten
boxing	Boxen
ice-skating	Schlittschuhlaufen
aerobics	Aerobic
swimming	Schwimmen
sailing	Segeln
riding	Reiten
golf	Golf
hockey	Hockey
judo	Judo

motor racing	Autorennen
parachuting	Fallschirm-springen
rollerblading, in-line skating	Inlineskating
hiking	Bergwandern
snowboarding	Snowboardfahren
climbing	Klettern
bowling	Bowlen
ballet	Ballett

to slip	ausrutschen
to wave	winken
to win	gewinnen
fit	fit, einsatzfähig
to take s.th. up	etwas beginnen
outdoor	draußen, Freiluft-

badminton

Olympics	olympische Spiele
Paralympics	Paralympische Spiele
World Championship	Weltmeisterschaft
Formula One	Formel 1

playing golf is an outdoor activity

word families:
to fence · *fencing*
to box · *boxing*
to swim · *swim* · *swimming*
to ride · *ride* · *riding*
to hike · *hike* · *hiking*
to climb · *climb* · *climbing*
to win · *winner*

irregular verbs:
to swim · swam · swum
to ride · rode · ridden
to win · won · won

Beispielsätze:

The greatest events in British motor racing happen at Silverstone.

For outdoor sports like climbing or hiking you need good equipment, for example slip-resistant boots.

If you want to take up rollerblading or skateboarding you need protection gear for your hands, wrists, knees and elbows. A lot of shops offer a combination of these protective pads.

Science and Technology

communication	Verständigung
telephone	Telefon
to phone	anrufen
mobile phone	Handy
to ring	anrufen
to call	anrufen
to dial	wählen, eintippen
phone card	Telefonkarte
telephone box	Telefonzelle
message	Mitteilung
fax machine	Faxgerät
to fax	per Faxgerät senden

mobile phone

computer / internet	Computer / Internet
PC	PC
word processor	Textverarbeitung
equipped	ausgerüstet
graphics	Bilder
laptop	Laptop
mouse mat	Mousepad
screen	Bildschirm
software	Software
data	Daten
to store	speichern
to function	funktionieren
to download	herunterladen
email	E-Mail
to link	verbinden
website	Website
virtual reality	virtuelle Realität

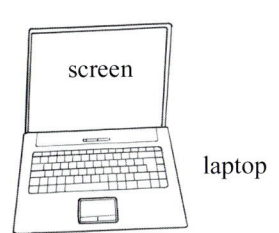

screen

laptop

specific	spezifisch
general	allgemein
relevant	bedeutsam
thick	dick
compact	kompakt
negative	negativ
positive	positiv
identical	identisch, genau gleich
possible	möglich

word families:
to phone · *phone*
to call · *call*
to equip · *equipment* · equipped
to function · *function*
relevance · relevant
to identify · *identity* · *identification*
possibility · possible

opposites:
thick↔thin
identical↔different

Beispielsätze: Can you phone me on my mobile phone later? If I don't answer, just leave a message or send me a text message.

Storing personal data must be handled more strictly, I think.
People ought to be more careful when they are asked specific details on the internet.

Science and Technology

entertainment	Unterhaltung
CD-player	CD-Spieler
headset	Kopfhörer
joystick	Steuerknüppel
stereo	Stereogerät
cassette	Kassette
CD	CD
hi-fi system	Stereoanlage
microphone	Mikrofon
radio	Radio
television (TV)	Fernseher
volume	Lautstärke

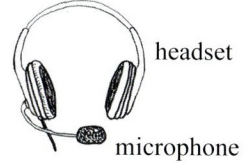

headset

microphone

radio

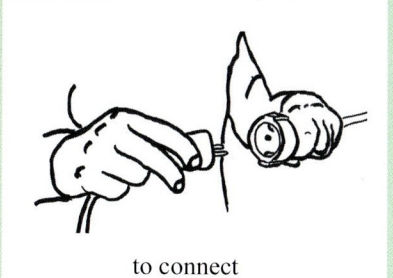

volume

television (TV)

to connect

to separate	trennen
material	Material
result	Ergebnis
to connect	verbinden
to drop	fallen lassen
similar	ähnlich
soft	weich

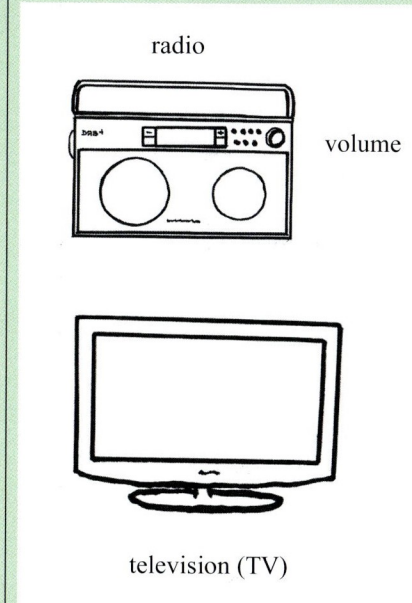

word families:

to visualise · *visualisation* · visual
to separate · *separation* · separate
to result (in) · *result*
to connect · *connection* · connected
similarity · similar

Beispielsätze: A lot of people spend their free time watching TV or surfing the internet.

Not long ago, people used video cassettes to watch films. Today we use DVDs.
They are much smaller and don't take up as much space on the shelf as the old video cassettes.

These results are very similar. They are almost the same.

Science and Technology

to invent	erfinden
ultrasound	Ultraschall
theory	Theorie
molecule	Molekül
research	Forschung
strategy	Taktik, Strategie
structure	Aufbau
iron	Eisen
to recycle	wiederaufbereiten

machinery	Maschinen (-anlagen)
grease	Schmierfett
motor, engine	Motor
locomotive	Lokomotive
turbine	Turbine
to switch on / off	an-/ausschalten
vibration	Schwingung
robot	Roboter

energy	Energie
to generate electricity	Energie erzeugen
generator	Generator
electrical	elektrisch
alternative sources	alternative Energiequellen
biofuel	biologischer Brennstoff
hydroelectric power	Wasserkraft
solar power	Sonnenenergie
solar panel	Sonnenkollektor
wind power	Windkraft
wind farms	Windparks
wind turbine	Windrad

to switch on / off

traditional sources	traditionelle Quellen
oil	Öl
nuclear power	Kernkraft
nuclear waste	Atommüll
coal	Kohle
gas	Gas

to suppose	annehmen, vermuten
to install	einbauen
to mix	mischen
to refer to	sich beziehen auf
special	besonders
to experience	eine Erfahrung machen, erfahren

word families:

to invent · *invention*
to vibrate · *vibration*
electricity · electrical
to install · *installation*
to mix · *mixture*
to refer · *reference*
to specialise · *speciality* · special
to experience · *experience*

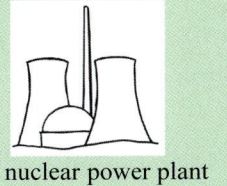

nuclear power plant

Beispielsätze:

wind turbine

Alexander Graham Bell invented the telephone in 1876.

Switch that engine off, please. It makes too much noise.

You can generate electricity with solar panels or with wind turbines, for example. One big advantage of these alternative sources is that they don't produce harmful waste like nuclear power plants. It is very important that we find safer and cleaner ways of obtaining electricity, especially after what happened in Fukushima. Our environment is too precious to be treated like that.

Science and Technology

science	Naturwissenschaft
chain	Kette
extreme	extrem, äußerst
chemical	chemisch
CFC	FCKW
ozone	Ozon
gas	Gas
oxygen	Sauerstoff
degree	Grad
to freeze	gefrieren, einfrieren
future	zukünftig
high-tech	Hochtechnologie
knowledge	Wissen, Kenntnis
laser	Laser
method	Verfahren
motion	Bewegung
observatory	Sternwarte
expert	Experte, Expertin

observatory

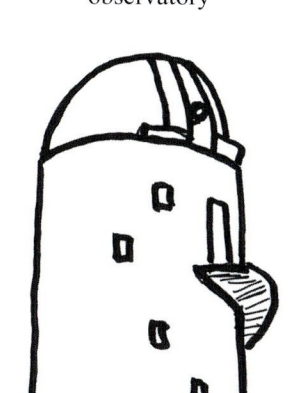

You can observe stars, planets and space objects from here.

protein	Protein
steam	Dampf
to try	versuchen
to experiment	experimentieren
plastic	Kunststoff
to clone	klonen
genetically modified	genetisch verändert
to innovate	Neuerungen einführen
system	System, Organismus
technical	technisch
electronic	elektronisch
to control	steuern, kontrollieren
to photocopy	fotokopieren
unpredictable	unvorhersagbar
instructions	Anweisungen
to test	prüfen, testen

word families:
science · *scientist* · scientific
future · futuristic
to know · *knowledge*
to try · *trial*
to experiment · *experiment*
to innovate · *innovation* · innovative
to control · *control*
to predict · *prediction* · predictable · unpredictable
to instruct · *instruction* · instructive

Beispielsätze: There is a hole in our planet's ozone layer. It is mainly caused by CFCs.

We must all help to protect our planet.
A lot of people are also worried about the use of genetically modified plants because the ecological consequences are unknown at present.

Geography

vast	riesig
to explore	erkunden
to orientate	sich orientieren
map	Landkarte
area	Gebiet
capital	Hauptstadt
town	Stadt
city	Stadt, Innenstadt, Großstadt
urban	städtisch
to inhabit	bewohnen
centre	Zentrum
ground	Boden
native	einheimisch
countryside	ländliche Gegend, Landschaft
rural	ländlich

continent	Erdteil, Kontinent
Asia	Asien
Europe	Europa
Africa	Afrika
America	Amerika
Australia	Australien
British Isles	Britische Inseln
Great Britain	Großbritannien
Ireland	Irland

mountain	Berg
top	Gipfel
bottom	Boden, unteres Ende
gorge	Schlucht
hill	Hügel
highlands	Hochland
valley	Tal

sea	Meer
ocean	Ozean
cliff	Klippe, Fels
coast	Küste
island	Insel
isle	Insel
peninsula	Halbinsel
river	Fluss
to flow	fließen
to meander	sich schlängeln
along	entlang, weiter
lake	See, Teich

direction	Richtung
north	Norden, nördlich
south	Süden, südlich
east	Osten, östlich
west	Westen, westlich

word families:
to explore · *exploration* · *explorer*
to orientate · *orientation*
to inhabit · *inhabitant*

synonyms:
vast ≈ huge
island ≈ isle

opposites:
urban↔rural
mountain↔valley
top↔bottom
north↔south
east↔west

Beispielsätze:
The Maori are the native population of New Zealand.
The British Isles consist of two main islands: Great Britain and Ireland.
Connemara is a beautiful region in Ireland. There are lovely hills, valleys, rivers and lakes.
The highest mountain in Scotland is Ben Nevis.
Thousands of tourists come to the Scottish Highlands every year.
The Scottish countryside is breathtaking.

Geography

countries in Europe (geographically)	Länder in Europa
Albania	Albanien
Andorra	Andorra
Austria	Österreich
Belarus	Weißrussland
Belgium	Belgien
Bosnia and Herzegovina	Bosnien und Herzegowina
Bulgaria	Bulgarien
Croatia	Kroatien
Cyprus	Zypern
Czech Republic	Tschechien
Denmark	Dänemark
Estonia	Estland
Finland	Finnland
France	Frankreich
Germany	Deutschland
Greece	Griechenland
Hungary	Ungarn

Iceland	Island
Ireland	Irland
Italy	Italien
Kosovo	Kosovo
Latvia	Lettland
Liechtenstein	Liechtenstein
Lithuania	Litauen
Luxembourg	Luxemburg
Macedonia	Mazedonien
Malta	Malta
Moldova	Moldawien
Monaco	Monaco
Montenegro	Montenegro
the Netherlands / Holland	Niederlande / Holland
Norway	Norwegen

Poland	Polen
Portugal	Portugal
Romania	Rumänien
Russia	Russland
San Marino	San Marino
Serbia	Serbien
Slovakia	Slowakei
Slovenia	Slowenien
Spain	Spanien
Sweden	Schweden
Switzerland	Schweiz
Turkey	Türkei
Ukraine	Ukraine
United Kingdom of Great Britain and Northern Ireland (UK)	Vereinigtes Königreich von Großbritannien und Nordirland
Vatican City	Vatikanstadt

Beispielsätze: Andorra is a microstate in the Pyrenees, near the French and Spanish border.
Hungary joined the EU in 2004.
The Netherlands are also called Holland.
Only 28 European countries are EU member states, Switzerland, for example, is not.
The UK consists of Great Britain (= England, Scotland, Wales) and Northern Ireland.

History

timeline	Zeitachse
slave	Sklave/Sklavin
master	Herr, Gebieter
civil war	Bürgerkrieg
revenge	Rache
Native Americans	Indianer
tribe	Stamm
chief	Häuptling
to settle	(be)siedeln
pioneer	Pionier
to fight	kämpfen
colony	Kolonie
treaty	Vertrag
to segregate	absondern, trennen
to discriminate	diskriminieren
freedom	Freiheit
independence	Unabhängigkeit
to found	(be-)gründen

Saxon	Sachse, sächsisch
Viking	Wikinger, wikingisch
Roman	Römer, römisch
Norman	Normanne, normannisch
to conquer	erobern
to fall	fallen
Middle Ages	Mittelalter
knight	Ritter
lance	Lanze
destruction	Zerstörung
fort	Festung
gold rush	Goldrausch
gold digger	Goldgräber
to abolish	abschaffen

citizen	Bürger
civil rights	Menschenrechte
protest	Protest
to protest	protestieren

knight

lance

word families:
slave · slavery
revenge · revengeful
to settle · settler
to fight · fight
to colonize · colony · colonial
to segregate · segregation · segregated
to discriminate · discrimination · discriminated
independence · independent
to found · founding · foundation
to conquer · conquered
to fall · fall
to destroy · destruction · destroyed
to abolish · abolishment · abolition · abolished
to protest · protest

opposites:
freedom↔slavery
dependence↔independence
to fall↔to rise

irregular verbs:
to fight · fought · fought
to fall · fell · fallen

Beispielsätze: In 1066 England was conquered by William I, Duke of Normandy, at the Battle of Hastings.

The first settlers from Europe came to the East coast of America and founded colonies.
The Sioux, the Cherokee or the Lakota are Native American tribes.
The US became independent in 1776.
In the 17th, 18th and 19th century slaves from Africa were brought to the US to work on plantations.
The Civil War was fought in America from 1861 to 1865. It finally ended slavery.

History

shield	Schild
bow	Bogen
arrow	Pfeil
famine	Hungersnot
to starve	verhungern
glorious	herrlich, glorreich
martyr	Märtyrer/in
legend	Legende
peace	Frieden
tower	Turm
origin	Ursprung

emperor	Kaiser
empress	Kaiserin
king	König
queen	Königin
prince	Prinz
princess	Prinzessin
earl	Graf
countess	Gräfin
duke	Herzog
duchess	Herzogin
nobleman	Adliger
noblewoman	Adlige

museum	Museum
weapon	Waffe
convict	Strafgefangene/r
warrior	Krieger/in
World War	Weltkrieg
apartheid	Rassentrennung (in Südafrika)

word families:
to starve · *starvation*
glory · glorious
peace · peaceful
to originate · *origin* · original

opposites:
peace↔war

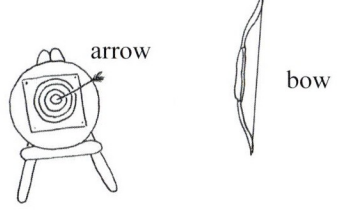
arrow
bow

Queen Elizabeth II

convict

Beispielsätze: Robin Hood, who used bows and arrows to shoot, is said to have lived in Sherwood Forest.
In the 19th century there was a great famine in Ireland. A lot of people starved to death because the potato crop failed.
In a monarchy the king or queen is the head of state.
In South Africa the apartheid regime ended after long negotiations and free elections.

Politics

state	Staat, Zustand
government	Regierung
opposition	Opposition
parliament	Parlament
MP (Member of Parliament)	Abgeordnete/r
Prime Minister	Premierminister/in

Downing Street No 10

House of Commons	Unterhaus
House of Lords	Oberhaus
minister	Minister/in

monarchy	Monarchie
royal	königlich
majesty	Majestät
to reign, to rule	regieren
throne	Thron

chancellor	Kanzler/in
speech	Rede
mayor	Bürgermeister/in
candidate	Kandidat/in
to vote	wählen
election	Wahl
to campaign	Wahlkampf machen
public	öffentlich
to pass a law	ein Gesetz verabschieden
to protest	protestieren

non-violent	gewaltfrei
revolution	Revolution
majority	Mehrheit
minority	Minderheit
nation	Nation
empire	Reich, Imperium, Kaiserreich
Commonwealth	Commonwealth, Nationengemeinschaft
declaration	Erklärung
independence	Unabhängigkeit
neutral	neutral

word families:
to govern · *government*
to reign · *reign*
to vote · *vote* · *voter*
to elect · *election* · elected
to campaign · *campaign*
to speak · *speech*
to protest · *protest*
to declare · *declaration*
independence · independent

opposites:
violent↔non-violent
majority↔minority

Beispielsätze:
The parliament in Germany is called "Bundestag".
Britain's Prime Minister lives at 10 Downing Street.
The UK has a constitutional monarchy. This means that the head of state is a monarch.
Queen Victoria reigned from 1837 until 1901.
In an election, people vote for the political candidates who will represent them.
The Commonwealth is an organisation of more than 50 states, mostly former territories of the British Empire.
The US gained its independence in 1776.

Politics

authority	Behörde
institution	Institution
republic	Republik
democracy	Demokratie
constitution	Verfassung
population	Bevölkerung
the people	das Volk
president	Präsident/in
legislature	gesetzgebende Gewalt, Gesetzgebung
congress	Kongress
senate	Senat
politician	Politiker/in
representative	Abgeordnete/r

party	Partei
conservative	konservativ
liberal	liberal
democratic	demokratisch
national	national
federal	bundesstaatlich

trade union	Gewerkschaft
to discuss	diskutieren
to debate	debattieren
leader	Führer/in
tax	Steuer
taxpayer	Steuerzahler/in
to include	beinhalten

national anthem	Nationalhymne
flag	Fahne

embassy	Botschaft
ambassador	Botschafter/in
asylum	Anstalt, Asyl
immigrant	Einwanderer/ Einwanderin
to immigrate	einwandern
to migrate	abwandern
to emigrate	auswandern
integration	Integration
migration	(Ab-)Wanderung
segregation	Rassentrennung

British national anthem

God save our gra-cious Queen long live our
no - ble Queen, God save the Queen.

word families:
to discuss · *discussion*
to debate · *debate*
to immigrate · *immigration* · *immigrant*
to migrate · *migration*
to emigrate · *emigration*
to integrate · *integration*
to segregate · *segregation*

opposites:
to immigrate↔to emigrate

Beispielsätze:
In democratic countries people are allowed to vote and are guaranteed human rights.
Before a law is passed there are often heated debates in parliament.

In the 18th and 19th centuries a lot of Irish people had to emigrate.
It is very hard to immigrate to the US today.
Before an international football match the national anthems of both teams are played in the stadium.

Nature and Environment

water	Wasser
sea	Meer
seaside	Küste
ocean	Ozean, Meer
wave	Welle
beach	Strand
sand	Sand
shore	Küste, Ufer
bay	Bucht
tides	Gezeiten
to surf	surfen
coast	Küste
island	Insel
lake	See
pond	Teich
river	Fluss
brook	Bach
waterfall	Wasserfall
to splash	spritzen
to swim	schwimmen

mountains	Berge, Gebirge
summit	Gipfel
hill	Hügel
rock	Fels
steep	steil
stone	Stein
avalanche	Lawine

earth	Erde
mud	Schlamm, Dreck
sandstone	Sandstein
desert	Wüste
moor	Moor, Hochmoor
prairie	Prärie, Grasebene
swampland	Sumpf(-gebiet)

parks and forests	Parks und Wälder
nature reserve	Naturschutzgebiet
ranger	Aufseher/in
wild	wild, unberührt
wilderness	Wildnis
tree	Baum
trunk	Baumstamm
log	Holzklotz, Holzscheit
oak	Eiche
pine	Kiefer
firewood	Brennholz
to fell	fällen
to burn	(an-)brennen
flame	Flamme
shade	Schatten
smoke	Rauch
grass	Gras
path	Pfad, Weg

word families:
nature · natural

opposites:
high tide↔low tide
mountain↔valley

irregular verbs:
to swim · swam · swum
to burn · burnt · burnt

Beispielsätze: I love being at the seaside / ... at the sea/ ... at the ocean.
Walking along the beach, watching the waves and feeling the sand under my feet is so relaxing.
You have to be careful with the tides, though.

Edmund Hillary was the first person to reach the summit of Mount Everest.

Nature and Environment

agriculture	Landwirtschaft
field	Feld, Acker
land	Boden, Acker, Grundstück
ground	Grund, Boden
vineyard	Weinberg
to grow	anpflanzen, wachsen
rural	ländlich
corn	Getreide
wheat	Weizen
barley	Gerste

village	Dorf
town	Stadt
suburb	Vorort
city	Stadt
port	Hafen, Hafenstadt

light	Licht
sun	Sonne
to rise	aufgehen
to set	untergehen
moon	Mond
star	Stern, Star
shine	scheinen
shadow	Schatten
dark	dunkel
darkness	Dunkelheit

garden	Garten
flower	Blume
bush	Busch
weed	Unkraut
shrub	Busch, Strauch
to blossom	blühen
leaf	Blatt
root	Wurzel

resources	Rohstoffquellen
fossil fuel	fossiler Brennstoff
coal	Kohle
oil	Öl
gas	Gas
geothermal	aus Erdwärme stammend
metal	Metall
silver	Silber
gold	Gold
diamond	Diamant

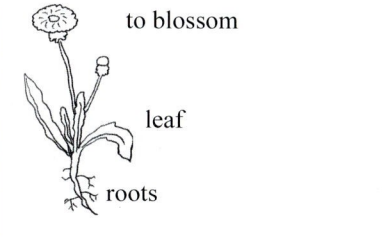

to blossom

leaf

roots

word families:
to blossom · *blossom*
to weed · *weed*
to root · *root* · rooted

opposites:
rural↔urban
suburb↔city-centre
light↔darkness
to rise↔to set
dark↔bright

irregular verbs:
to grow · grew · grown
to rise · rose · risen
to shine · shone · shone

irregular plurals:
leaf · leaves

Beispielsätze: There are a lot of vineyards in the South of France. It is a wine-growing region.
The sun rises in the east and sets in the west.
Apple trees blossom in April or May.
You can see your shadow when the sun shines.

Nature and Environment

pollution	Umweltver-schmutzung
emissions	Abgase
contaminated	verschmutzt
household waste	Hausmüll
litter	Abfall
pesticide	Pestizid
to pollute	verschmutzen
radioactive waste	radioaktiver Abfall
rubbish	Abfall, Müll
smog	Smog
noise	Lärm
toxic	giftig
to leak	lecken, auslaufen
to endanger	gefährden
to dump	abladen
acid rain	saurer Regen

loud	laut
silent	ruhig, still
rare	selten
real	wirklich
slippery	rutschig
tiny	winzig
necessary	notwendig
essential	entscheidend, wesentlich

radioactive waste

toxic

effect	Effekt
greenhouse gases	Treibhausgase

consequences	Folgen
hole in the ozone layer	Ozonloch
global warming	Erderwärmung
climate change	Klimawandel
drought	Dürre
dry	trocken
flood	Flut, Überschwemmung
glacier retreat	Rückgang der Gletscher
to melt	schmelzen
rising sea levels	Anstieg der Meeresspiegel

word families:
to contaminate ·
contamination ·
contaminated
silence · silent
reality · real · realistic
to pollute · *pollution* ·
polluted
to leak · *leak* · leaking

opposites:
loud↔quiet/ silent
real↔unreal
tiny↔giant
necessary↔unnecessary
dry↔wet

Beispielsätze: Our environment is endangered.
Emissions, household waste, pesticides and radioactive waste pollute our planet.
Greenhouse gases warm the climate and cause global warming.
This climate change affects weather patterns, leading to more floods, droughts and bush fires.
More powerful and dangerous hurricanes will also occur, scientists say.

Animals and Insects

wildlife	wildlebende Tiere
bear	Bär
polar bear	Eisbär
hedgehog	Igel
badger	Dachs
deer	Reh, Rotwild
mouse, mice	Maus, Mäuse
koala	Koalabär
kangaroo	Känguru
elephant	Elefant
lion	Löwe
zebra	Zebra
tiger	Tiger
monkey	Affe
buffalo	Büffel, Bison
reptiles	Reptilien
crocodile	Krokodil
snake	Schlange
turtle	Wasserschildkröte
tortoise	Landschildkröte

insects	Insekten
ant	Ameise
beetle	Käfer
bee	Biene
fly	Fliege
butterfly	Schmetterling

Sheep are farm animals.

farm animals	Nutztiere
cattle	Rinder, Vieh
cow	Kuh
ox	Ochse
bull	Bulle, Stier
sheep (sg+pl)	Schaf, Schafe
sheepdog	Hirtenhund
lamb	Lamm
pig	Schwein
hen	Henne
rooster	Hahn
donkey	Esel
goose, geese	Gans, Gänse
turkey	Truthahn
horse	Pferd
pony	Pony
goat	Ziege
duck	Ente
rabbit	Kaninchen

irregular plurals:
mouse · mice
calf · calves
sheep · sheep
ox · oxen
goose · geese

geese

polar bear

Beispielsätze:
The polar bear is a threatened species.
A lot of the sea ice is melting and its natural habitat is endangered.
Elephants are well known for their intelligence, close family ties and social complexity.
Many people don't like reptiles such as snakes or crocodiles.
Most farm animals have a hard life on factory farms.
They often lack space, fresh air or daylight.

Animals and Insects

birds	Vögel
eagle	Adler
falcon	Falke
pigeon	Taube
owl	Eule
penguin	Pinguin

dolphins

sea animals	Meerestiere
dolphin	Delphin
whale	Wal
fish	Fisch
shark	Hai
seal	Robbe

shark

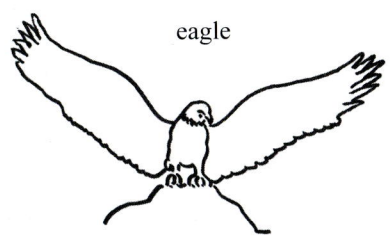

eagle

pets	Haustiere
dog	Hund
budgie	Wellensittich
guinea pig	Meerschweinchen
cat	Katze
goldfish	Goldfisch
hamster	Hamster

to feed	füttern
to bark	bellen
to wag the tail	mit dem Schwanz wedeln
to purr	schnurren

irregular plurals:
one fish · two fish

irregular verbs:
to feed · fed · fed

Beispielsätze:

Allan feeds his dog twice a day.
Dogs bark to warn their owners.
When a dog is happy it wags its tail.
Cats often purr.

Weather

wind	Wind
windy	windig
to blow	blasen
breeze	Brise
rain	Regen
cloud	Wolke
to cloud over	trüb werden
snow	Schnee
ice	Eis
frost	Frost
cold	kalt
to freeze	gefrieren
chilly	kühl, frisch
sun	Sonne
to shine	scheinen
hot	heiß
warm	warm
sunny	sonnig
heat	Hitze

storm	Sturm
hurricane	Hurrikan
tornado	Wirbelsturm, Tornado
blizzard	Schneesturm
thunderstorm	Gewitter
thunder	Donner
lightning	Blitz
umbrella	Regenschirm
waterproofs	wasserabweisende Kleidung
rain gear	Regenkleidung
fog	Nebel
mist, haze	feiner Nebel, Dunst
hail	Hagel
sunny spells	sonnige Abschnitte

air	Luft
haze	Dunst
fog	Nebel
sky	Himmel

cloudy with sunny spells

rain

word families:
wind · windy
to rain · *rain* · rainy
to cloud over · *cloud* · cloudy
to snow · *snow*
to hail · *hail*
fog · foggy

irregular verbs:
to blow · blew · blown
to freeze · froze · frozen
to shine · shone · shone

Beispielsätze: At the sea it is often windy. It can get quite chilly in autumn.
You need to be very careful when there is snow or ice on the road.
A blizzard is a severe snow storm.
Take an umbrella with you, it might rain this afternoon.
There will be sunny spells in the South-East of England later in the day.
When it is foggy, you can hardly see your hand in front of your face.
Look at my car, it got damaged in the hail storm yesterday.

Working World / Application

application	Bewerbung
to accept	annehmen
ambition	Ehrgeiz, Ziel
appearance	Aussehen
to employ	beschäftigen
experienced	erfahren
including	einschließlich
apprentice	Lehrling
career	Berufsweg
interviewer	Leiter/in des Vorstellungsgesprächs
contract	Vertrag
CV	Lebenslauf
available	verfügbar
to fill in	ausfüllen
in writing	schriftlich

to enclose	beilegen
formal	formell
intern (A.E.)	Praktikant/in
trainee (B.E.)	Praktikant/in, Auszubildende/r
to reply	antworten
work experience	Berufserfahrung, Praktikum
skill	Fertigkeit, Fähigkeit
opportunity	Gelegenheit
point	Punkt
quality	Qualität
controlled	kontrolliert
convenient	passend
to bring	bringen

Karen Schulz
Am Anger 12
80331 München
Tel. +49 89 534324367
K.Schulz@t-online.de

April 12, 2015

Mr Brian Daly
Natural History Museum
Cromwell Road
London
SW7 5BD
UK

Dear Mr Daly

Application for a volunteer position

I am writing to apply for the volunteer position which was advertised in The Guardian on Tuesday 31 March 2015, and I enclose my CV in application.
As you will see from my CV I have just graduated from …
I look forward to meeting you.

Yours sincerely,
…

word families:
to apply · *application*
to accept · *acceptance* · acceptable
to appear · *appearance*
to employ · *employer* · *employee*
experience · experienced
to include · including
apprentice · *apprenticeship*
to interview · *interviewer*
to enclose · *enclosed*
intern · *internship*
to reply · *reply*
to control · *control*
convenience · convenient

synonyms:
opportunity ≈ chance
convenient ≈ suitable

opposites:
available↔unavailable
formal↔informal

irregular verbs:
to bring · brought · brought

Beispielsätze: This job that the BBC is advertising is a great opportunity for Sally. She has to hand in her application and a CV by the end of July. I know that her greatest ambition is to become a reporter. At the moment she is employed at a local radio station. I think that in an interview she would be asked about her work experience and her career plans. The job at the BBC would be very convenient for her because she could go to work by bus. She only lives two stops away.

Working World / Application

to delay	verschieben, verzögern
to insist on	bestehen auf
to knock	klopfen
to relate to	sich beziehen auf
to roll	rollen
to criticize	kritisieren
to end	beenden
to expect	erwarten

to spray	sprühen
to suggest	vorschlagen
to introduce	vorstellen
to manage to do s.th.	es schaffen, etwas zu tun, etwas fertig bringen
to persuade	überreden
to reclaim	zurückverlangen
to put	legen, stellen, setzen

to shut	schließen
to pump	pumpen
to push	schieben
to recommend	empfehlen
to simplify	vereinfachen
knot	Knoten

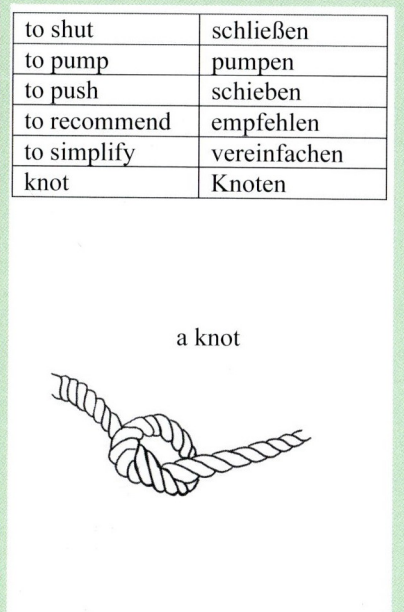

a knot

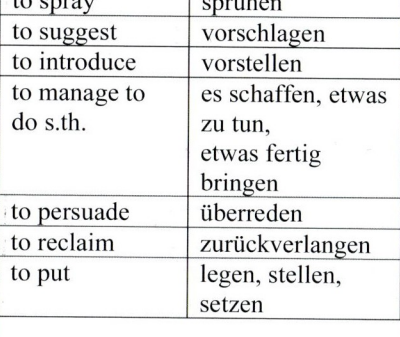

MANAGER

to knock

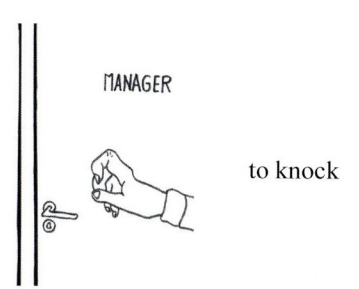

to spray

Beispielsätze: It is not always easy to explain to customers that the delivery has been delayed.
Some insist on cancelling their order, which is within their rights.
They expect to get their goods in time, which is understandable.

word families:
to delay · *delay* · delayed
to knock · *knock*
to relate (to) · *relation* · related
to criticize · *criticism* · critic · critical
to end · *end*
to expect · *expectation*
to suggest · *suggestion*
to introduce · *introduction*
to manage · *manager*
to persuade · *persuasion* · persuasive
to reclaim · *reclamation* · reclaimable
to pump · *pump*
to recommend · *recommendation* · recommended
to simplify · *simplification* · simplified

synonyms:
to end ≈ to finish
to shut ≈ to close

opposites:
to criticize↔to praise
to end↔to start
to shut↔to open
to push↔to pull
to simplify↔to complicate

irregular verbs:
to put · put · put
to shut · shut · shut

Money and Business

bank	Bank
cash machine	Geldautomat
credit	Kredit
credit card	Kreditkarte
code	Kennzahl
fee	Gebühr
currency	Währung
share	Aktie, Anteil
to speculate	spekulieren
to trade	Handel treiben
bargain	Schnäppchen
to borrow s.th.	sich etwas ausleihen
to lend	verleihen
debt(s)	Schuld(-en)
interest rate	Zinssatz
to increase	sich vermehren
to save	sichern, sparen
cash	Bargeld, Geld

to spend	ausgeben
money	Geld
coin	Münze
bill	Rechnung, Geldschein
cent	Cent
pence (pl)	Pfennige
penny	Pfennig

a fifty dollar bill

firm	Firma
enterprise	Unternehmen
business	Geschäft
entrepreneur	Unternehmer/in
cash register	Registrierkasse
earnings	Einkünfte
to export	exportieren, ausführen
to import	einführen
goods	Waren
marketable	gut zu vermarkten
to file	ablegen, abheften

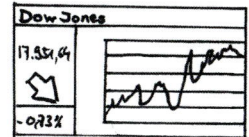

word families:
to speculate · *speculation* · *speculative*
to trade · *trade* · *trader*
to increase · *increase*
to save · *safe* · *savings* · safe
to earn · *earnings*
to export · *export*
to file · *file*

synonyms:
firm ≈ company

opposites:
to borrow↔to lend
to increase↔to decrease
to save↔to spend
to export↔to import

irregular verbs:
to lend · lent · lent
to spend · spent · spent

Beispielsätze:
I can lend you 10 pounds. (You lend s.th. **to** someone)
Can I borrow your bicycle? (You borrow s.th. **from** somebody)
Germany exports a lot of goods to other European countries.
Can I pay by credit card?
I am sorry, we only take VISA or Master Card.
The currency of the US is the US dollar.
People who are in debt must often pay high interest rates to the bank.

Money and Business

to offer	anbieten
to sell	verkaufen
profit	Gewinn
consultant	Berater/in
to deliver	liefern
parcel	Paket
economy	Wirtschaft
to expand	erweitern
to guarantee	garantieren
product	Produkt
guard	Wache
per cent	Prozent
promotion	Beförderung, Werbung

%　per cent

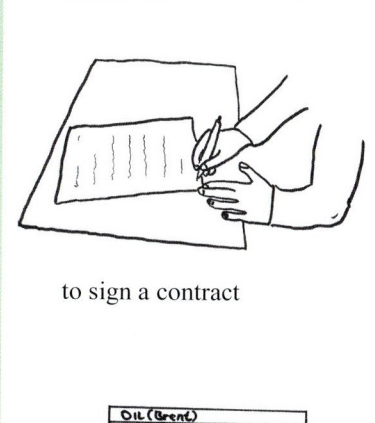

to sign a contract

mainly	hauptsächlich
professional	fachgerecht, professionell
regular	regelmäßig
to keep	behalten
to reach	reichen
increasingly	ansteigend, zunehmend
to reduce	vermindern
to sign (a contract)	(einen Vertrag) unterschreiben
Yours sincerely	Mit freundlichen Grüßen
spokesperson	Sprecher/in
statistics	Statistik(-en)

Beispielsätze:　Jerome sold his house and made a huge profit.
He got 50, 000 dollars more than he had paid for it ten years ago.

In business there is often pressure to expand quickly.
If you want to increase your profits, one way is to invent new products.

Social Problems

unemployment	Arbeitslosigkeit
to cope with	fertig werden mit, bewältigen, meistern
to depend on	abhängig sein von
difficulty	Schwierigkeit
choice	Wahl
to complain about	sich beschweren über
boredom	Langeweile
problem	Problem
reason	Grund, Ursache
reasonable	vernünftig, angemessen

homelessness	Obdachlosigkeit
to discriminate against	diskriminieren
to fit in	dazu passen, sich einfügen
to hang around	herumhängen
severe	streng, hart
dirty	schmutzig
shack	Hütte, Schuppen

Homeless people often sleep on the streets.

drug abuse	Drogenmissbrauch
cannabis	Haschisch
ecstasy	Ecstasy
impossible	unmöglich
drug	Droge, Medikament
soft drug	weiche Droge
gang	Gang, Bande
risk	Risiko
trouble	Ärger

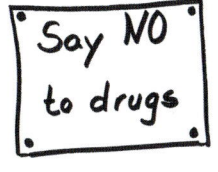

Say NO to drugs

word families:
unemployment · unemployed
to depend · *dependence* · dependent
difficulty · difficult
to choose · *choice*
to complain · *complaint*
boredom · bored
reason · reasonable
homelessness · homeless
to discriminate · *discrimination* · discriminated
to risk · *risk* · risky

opposites:
dirty↔clean
possible↔impossible

Beispielsätze: A country with a high unemployment rate has widespread social and economic problems. People who lose their jobs need financial and often also social help. A lot of them don't like being dependent on the state.

Severe drug abuse often leads to serious problems, such as homelessness. People who can't pay their rent anymore often end up sleeping on the streets.

Social Problems

to wish	wünschen
worried	besorgt
bad	schlecht
tough	hart, widerstandsfähig
trapped	gefangen, in der Falle sitzend
to support	unterstützen
to wonder	sich fragen
to offer	anbieten
to share	teilen
unfortunately	leider, bedauerlicherweise

to offer help

solution	Lösung
disgusting	widerlich, abscheulich
sympathy	Mitgefühl
unbelievable	unglaublich
to cling	klammern, haften
to be unlucky	Pech haben
to give	geben
uncomfortable	unbequem

word families:
to worry · *worry* · worried
to trap s.o. · *trap* · trapped
to support · *support* · supported
to offer · *offer*
to share · *share*
to solve · *solution* · solved
to sympathize · *sympathy* · sympathetic

synonyms:
tough ≈ hard
to wonder ≈ to ask oneself
disgusting ≈ abominable

opposites:
good↔bad
free↔trapped
lucky↔unlucky
to give↔to take
comfortable↔uncomfortable

irregular verbs:
to cling · clung · clung
to give · gave · given

Beispielsätze: I often wonder why people end up living on the streets. Unfortunately, their numbers seem to be growing. Charity organisations offer help and try to support them but it is hard to find solutions to their problems.

Social Problems

poverty	Armut
beggar	Bettler/in
poor	arm, schlecht
bankrupt	pleite, bankrott
burden	Belastung, Last
disadvantaged	benachteiligt
hunger	Hunger
miserable	elend, armselig
pitiful	mitleiderregend

to beg

to starve	verhungern
to suffer	leiden, erleiden
condition	Verfassung, Lage
rations	(Essens-) Rationen

discrimination	Diskriminierung
racism	Rassismus
riot	Aufstand
disadvantage	Nachteil
downside	Kehrseite, Nachteil
foreign	ausländisch
intolerable	unerträglich
prejudice	Vorurteil
stereotype	Klischeevorstellung
to tolerate	dulden, tolerieren
unfair	ungerecht
unfriendly	unfreundlich

help	Hilfe
to advise	(be-)raten
aspect	Aspekt, Seite
to avoid	(ver-)meiden
association	Vereinigung
to benefit	profitieren
care	Sorge, Pflege
social worker	Sozialarbeiter
sufficient	ausreichend
charity	Wohltätigkeit, wohltätige Organisation
community	Gemeinschaft
insurance	Versicherung
member	Mitglied
to provide with	versorgen mit
to raise (money)	(Geld) aufbringen
foster home	Pflegestelle
to get rid of	loswerden
to handle	umgehen mit
to hope	hoffen

word families:
poverty · poor
misery · miserable
to starve · *starvation*
to suffer · *suffering*
to advise · *advice*
to associate · *association* · associated
to benefit · *benefit* · beneficial
to care · *care* · caring · careful
sufficiency · sufficient
to insure · *insurance* · insured
to hope · *hope* · hopeful

synonyms:
sufficient ≈ enough

opposites:
advantage↔disadvantage
tolerable↔intolerable
fair↔unfair
friendly↔unfriendly
sufficient↔insufficient

irregular verbs:
to get (rid of) · got · got

Beispielsätze: More than 46 million Americans live in poverty, according to the organisation "Poverty USA".
Children who come from poor families often don't have the same chances as other children. When money is short, parents worry about how to pay the rent, and to pay for food, heating or health insurance. It is very difficult for them to handle all these problems.

Transport and Tourism

vehicle	Fahrzeug
car	Auto
helicopter	Hubschrauber
motorbike	Motorrad
van	Lieferwagen
campervan	Wohnmobil
boat	Boot
ship	Schiff
ferry	Fähre
taxi (B.E.)	Taxi
cable car	Seilbahn
bus	Bus, Linienbus
coach	Bus, Reisebus
tram	Straßenbahn
lorry (B.E.)	Lastwagen
underground (B.E.)	U-Bahn
subway (A.E.)	U-Bahn
double decker	Doppeldeckerbus
bus stop	Bushaltestelle
conductor	Schaffner/in

train	Zug
railway	Eisenbahn
station	Bahnhof
compartment	Abteil
plane	Flugzeug
to fly	fliegen
airport	Flughafen
arrival	Ankunft
departure	Abflug
boarding pass	Bordkarte
flight attendant	Flugbegleiter(in)
pilot	Pilot/in
timetable	Stundenplan, Fahrplan
terminal	Terminal
runway	Start- und Landebahn

bicycle	Fahrrad
to cycle	Fahrrad fahren
pedal	Pedal
handlebars	Lenkstange
pump	Luftpumpe
to ride a bike	Fahrrad fahren
to drive	fahren
to accelerate	beschleunigen
to speed	schnell fahren, rasen
to brake	bremsen
petrol (B.E.)	Benzin
boot (B.E.)	Kofferraum
steering wheel	Lenkrad
tyre	Reifen
windscreen (B.E.)	Windschutzscheibe
to overtake	überholen
wheel	Rad
to fasten one's seatbelt	sich anschnallen

word families:
to fly · *flight*
to arrive · *arrival*
to depart · *departure*
to drive · *driver*
to accelerate · *acceleration*
to get petrol · *petrol*

irregular verbs:
to drive · drove · driven
to overtake · overtook · overtaken
to fly · flew · flown

Beispielsätze:
My father owns three vehicles. He has a car, a motorbike and a campervan.
He doesn't speed because my mother hates it when he has to brake suddenly.
Before driving you should always fasten your seatbelt.

I love flying and I love the atmosphere at airports.
In the arrival hall it is great to watch all the people waiting for friends or relatives.

Transport and Tourism

bend	Kurve
to turn	abbiegen
crossing	Kreuzung
crossroads	Kreuzung
lane	Weg, Fahrspur
motorway	Autobahn
street	Straße
road	Straße, Landstraße
roundabout	Kreisverkehr
sign	Schild, Zeichen
zebra crossing	Zebrastreifen

lost property office	Fundbüro
travel insurance	Reiseversicherung
to get lost	verloren gehen, sich verlaufen

to ask the way	nach dem Weg fragen
to tell the way	den Weg beschreiben

to tell the way

luggage	Gepäck
suitcase	Koffer
bag	Tasche
backpack (A.E.)	Rucksack

to get on /off	ein-/aussteigen
fare	Fahrpreis
ticket	Fahrkarte
return ticket	Rückfahrkarte
to take off	starten
journey	Fahrt, Reise
trip	Ausflug, Reise
voyage	Seereise
to travel	reisen
to cruise	eine Seereise machen, herumfahren
beach	Strand
to sunbathe	sich sonnen
suntan	Sonnenbräune

suitcase

bag

word families:
to cross · *crossing* · *crossroads*

opposites:
to get on↔to get off
to take off↔to land

backpack

Beispielsätze:
Paul got on the number 87 bus. There he found a wallet.
He got off at Ellington Road. He wanted to book a holiday at the travel agency there.
First he wanted to hand the wallet in at the lost property office, which was near there.
Unfortunately, he got lost, but a nice shop assistant helped him and told him the way.
At the travel agency he booked a holiday to the Mediterranean.
He loves sunbathing and always gets a suntan quite easily.

Transport and Tourism

arranging a holiday	einen Urlaub organisieren
to book	buchen
travel agency	Reisebüro
guide	Reiseführer/in
guided tour	geführte Tour, Stadtführung
sightseeing	Besichtigung von Sehenswürdigkeiten
sight	Sehenswürdigkeit. Anblick, Sicht
destination	Ziel
brochure	Prospekt
cancellation	Stornierung
to tour	besichtigen, besuchen
to hire	mieten
tourist	Tourist/in

reception

accommodation	Unterkunft
to stay	wohnen, bleiben
B&B	Übernachtung mit Frühstück
hostel	Herberge
youth hostel	Jugendherberge
self-catering	mit Selbstversorgung
warden	Leiter/in der Jugendherberge, Herbergsvater
hotel	Hotel
chambermaid	Zimmermädchen
reception	Rezeption
campsite (B.E)	Campingplatz
campground (A.E.)	Campingplatz
tent	Zelt
to go camping	zelten
sleeping bag	Schlafsack

word families:
to guide · *guide* · guided
to cancel · *cancellation*

opposites:
to stay↔to leave

Beispielsätze: Brenda has arranged our holiday. She has booked a sightseeing tour around Cardiff. It is a guided tour by bus.
She has also hired a car so we can go on a tour of Wales later. We are going to stay in B&Bs because they are cheaper than hotel rooms. Camping would be the cheapest, but I hate sleeping in a tent.

Buildings and Housing / Household

buildings	Gebäude
flat	Wohnung
apartment	Wohnung
house	Haus
detached house	freistehendes Haus
semi-detached house	Doppelhaushälfte
terraced house	Reihenhaus
bungalow	Bungalow
skyscraper	Wolkenkratzer
castle	Burg, Schloss
villa	Villa
tower	Turm
cathedral	Kathedrale
town hall	Rathaus
stable	Stall
shed	Schuppen, Stall

rooms	Zimmer
bathroom	Badezimmer
kitchen	Küche
bedroom	Schlafzimmer
hall	Diele, Flur
living room	Wohnzimmer
toilet	Toilette
shower	Dusche

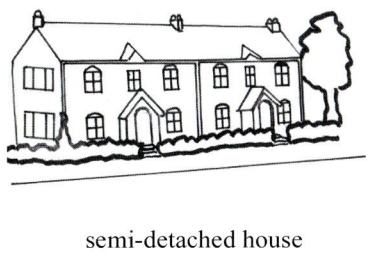

semi-detached house

to rent	mieten
downstairs	unten
upstairs	oben
roof	Dach
front door	Haustür
key	Schlüssel
garden	Garten
lawn	Rasen
veranda	Terrasse

detached house

word families:
to rent · *rent* · rented

opposites:
downstairs↔upstairs
front door↔back door

Beispielsätze:
Irene has rented a flat in Kensington. It is lovely.
We can't really afford a detached house in London, so we just bought a terraced house.
Downstairs is the kitchen and the living room, upstairs we have three bedrooms.
There is a lawn at the front of the house and a garden at the back.

Buildings and Housing / Household

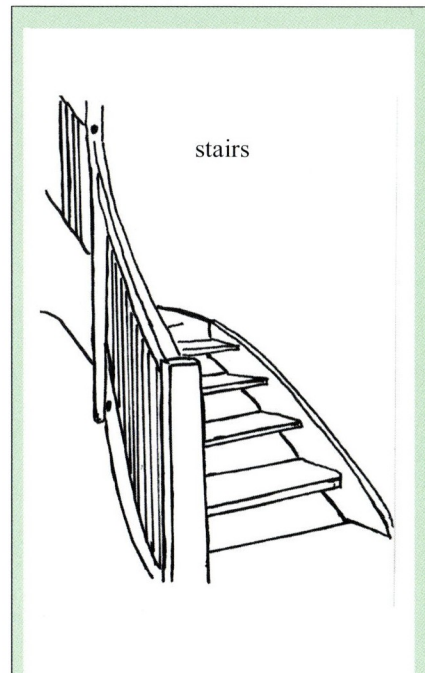

stairs

wall	Wand, Mauer
window	Fenster
to own	besitzen
floor	Etage, Boden
stairs	Treppe, Treppenhaus
step	Stufe, Schritt
entrance	Eingang
garage	Garage
gate	Tor

to hang a picture on the wall

edge	Ecke
tidy	ordentlich
untidy	unordentlich
to settle down	sich niederlassen
to hang a picture on the wall	ein Bild an die Wand hängen
to modernize	modernisieren
to switch on / off	ein-/ ausschalten
to lay	legen, setzen, stellen
to open	öffnen
to close	schließen

word families:
to own · *owner*
to tidy up · tidy
to modernize ·
modernization · modern
to switch on · *switch*
to open · *opening* · open
to close · *closure* · *closing* ·
closed

synonyms:
to close ≈ to shut
to lay ≈ to put
opposites:
tidy↔untidy
to switch on↔to switch off
to open↔to close

Beispielsätze:
We are going to modernize our shop-front.
What do you think about hanging some new pictures on the walls?
Would you please switch on the light for me?
Could you open the door, please?
We bought an old house in the country, but it will need modernization before we move in.

Buildings and Housing / Household

furniture	Möbel
bed	Bett
pillow	Kopfkissen
shelf, shelves	Regal, Regale
carpet	Teppich
desk	Schreibtisch
drawer	Schublade
wardrobe	Kleiderschrank
cupboard	Schrank
curtain	Vorhang
lampshade	Lampenschirm
mirror	Spiegel
table	Tisch
sofa	Sofa
lamp	Lampe
candle	Kerze
needle	Nadel
to sew	nähen
ladder	Leiter
fridge	Kühlschrank

bin	Mülleimer
rubbish	Abfall
oven	Backofen
pan	Pfanne
scissors	Schere
glass	Glas
plug	Stöpsel, Stecker
to plug in	einstöpseln
socket	Steckdose
brush	Bürste, Besen
bucket	Eimer

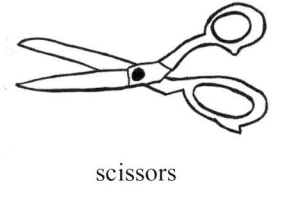

scissors

to cut	schneiden
sharp	scharf
to break	brechen
to mend	reparieren
to wash the dishes	Geschirr abwaschen
to dust	abstauben
to wipe	(ab-)wischen
to clean	putzen
to tidy up	aufräumen
to sweep	fegen
to vacuum	Staub saugen
to wash	waschen
washing machine	Waschmaschine
to iron	bügeln
ironing board	Bügelbrett
to peel	schälen
to spill	verschütten
to consume	verbrauchen

word families:
to cut · *cut* · cut
to dust · *dust* · dusty
to clean · *cleaning* · clean
to wash · *washing* · washed
to iron · *ironing* · ironed
to peel · *peel* · peeled
to consume · *consumption*

opposites:
to break↔to mend

irregular verbs:
to sew · sewed · sewn
to cut · cut · cut
to sweep · swept · swept

plural word:
scissors

Beispielsätze:
We have moved into our new house, but still need a few things, like shelves, carpets and lampshades.
We have already bought a comfortable sofa and a big wardrobe for all my clothes.
Where are my scissors? I think they are in the drawer.

Allan loves housework. He doesn't mind washing the dishes or tidying up the living room.
I hate vacuuming and ironing. It is so boring.

Newspapers, TV and Radio

newspaper	Zeitung
magazine	Zeitschrift
to print	drucken
article	Zeitungsartikel
to comment	kommentieren
daily	täglich
to influence	beeinflussen
theme, topic	Thema
headline	Schlagzeile
to inform	benachrichtigen
layout	Anordnung, Layout
popular press	Boulevardpresse
to popularize	populär machen
to publish	veröffentlichen
ad, advert, advertisement	Werbeanzeige, Werbung

TV	Fernsehen
radio	Radio
to broadcast	senden
commercial	Werbespot
slogan	Wahlspruch, Werbespruch
network	Sendenetz, Netz
sensation	Aufsehen, Sensation
series	Serie
soap	Seifenoper
viewer	Zuschauer/in
focus	Blickfeld, Zentrum
to interview	interviewen
news	Nachricht(en)
news item	Meldung
live	live, direkt
to press	drücken
channel	Kanal

to record	aufnehmen
weather forecast	Wettervorhersage
programme	Sendung, Programm
documentary	Dokumentarfilm
journalist	Journalist
to report	berichten

headline

word families:
to comment · *comment*
to influence · *influence*
to inform · *information*
to publish · *publisher*
to advertise · *advertisement*
to view · *viewer*
to interview · *interview*
to record · *recording* · recorded
to report · *report* · *reporter*

opposites:
live ↔ recorded

irregular verbs:
to broadcast · broadcast · broadcast

Beispielsätze:
The article on climate change was published in the Guardian.
It informed about the possibilities of cutting down on CO2 emissions.
Even the popular press regularly reports about the problems linked to climate change.
Hardly anyone denies that we must find solutions to these problems.

Have you seen the programme which shows the year's best commercials?
Some of them are fantastic.
No, I missed it. I watched a documentary on the BBC last night.

Law and order / Crime

to accuse	anklagen, beschuldigen
to blame	die Schuld geben
to admit	zugeben
to deny	leugnen
to find out	herausfinden
to enquire	sich erkundigen
evidence	Beweis, Indiz
to fine	Bußgeld verhängen
allowed	erlaubt
to look for	suchen
reward	Belohnung
legal	gesetzmäßig
matter	Angelegenheit
clue	Hinweis
hint	Tipp
to prove	beweisen
crime	Verbrechen

court	Gericht
judge	Richter/in
law	Gesetz
lawyer	Anwalt/Anwältin
to defend	verteidigen
true	wahr
to lose	verlieren
trial	Prozess
guilty	schuldig
innocent	unschuldig
witness	Zeuge, Zeugin
sentence	Strafe, Urteil
to sentence to death	zum Tode verurteilen
prison	Gefängnis
offence	Straftat
right	richtig; Recht
freedom	Freiheit

At court everyone should be treated in the same way, no matter how wealthy or influential he or she is.

word families:
to accuse · *accusation* · accused
to blame · *blame*
to enquire · *enquiry*
to fine · *fine*
to allow · *allowance* · allowed
to reward · *reward* · rewarding
to prove · *proof*
crime · criminal
to defend · *defence*
to judge · *judge*
truth · true
to lose · *loss*
guilt · guilty
innocence · innocent
to witness · *witness*
to sentence · *sentence*
to offend s.o. · *offence*
to free s.o. · *freedom* · free

opposites:
to admit↔to deny
to look for↔to find
legal↔illegal
true↔false
to lose↔to win
guilty↔innocent
right↔wrong

irregular verbs:
to find (out) · found · found
to lose · lost · lost

Beispielsätze: A 38-year-old man was arrested in Croydon yesterday.
Police think that he stole a car from a car park.
He has a record for selling stolen cars.
So far, the man hasn't been proved guilty.
He claims to be innocent.
He admitted having been at the car park, but denied having anything to do with the car theft.
There are no witnesses.
There will be a trial in which the truth will hopefully be found out.

Law and order / Crime

to arrest someone	jmdn. verhaften
permission	Erlaubnis
safety	Sicherheit
to guard	bewachen
security	Sicherheit
cause	Ursache, Grund

police	Polizei
metal detector	Metallsuchgerät
police officer	Polizist, Polizistin
cop (A.E.)	Polizist/in
police station	Polizeirevier
to question	befragen
to protect	beschützen
to release	freilassen
to suspect	verdächtigen

to chase	verfolgen, jagen
danger	Gefahr
detective	Detektiv
detail	Einzelheit
to escape	flüchten
to follow	(ver-)folgen
to identify	identifizieren
incident	Vorfall, Ereignis
to lock	abschließen
to solve	lösen (ein Problem)
to investigate	untersuchen, ermitteln

British police officer

mystery	Geheimnis
pirate	Pirat/in
to plan	planen
to scream	schreien
plot	Verschwörung
secret	geheim, Geheimnis
shocking	schockierend
to stab	niederstechen
trick	Trick
valuable	wertvoll
to reveal sth.	etw. enthüllen

detective

Beispielsätze: Nelson Mandela was released from prison after 27 years and became the first black President of South Africa in 1994.
He spent 18 of the 27 years on Robben Island, where a new cell block had been constructed for political prisoners.
It was impossible to escape from there.

Law and order / Crime

alarm	Alarm
to capture	fangen
to arrest	festnehmen
handcuffs	Handschellen
breathalyser	Promillemesser
pistol	Pistole
gun	Schusswaffe
revolver	Revolver
rifle	Gewehr
to shoot	schießen
cannon	Kanone

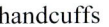

handcuffs

bullet	Geschoss, Kugel
explosion	Explosion
fireball	Feuerball
to explode	explodieren
to blow up	in die Luft jagen
to bomb	bombardieren
to fire	schießen, feuern

It is going to explode in a minute.

burglar	Einbrecher/in
robber	Räuber/in
mugger	Straßenräuber/in
to break (into)	(ein-)brechen
to steal	stehlen
thief, thieves	Dieb/in, Diebe/ Diebinnen
fake	Fälschung
to fight	kämpfen
to flee	fliehen
to free	freilassen

burglar

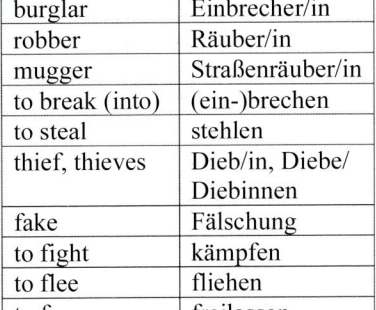

word families:
to arrest· *arrest*
to shoot· *shot*
to explode· *explosion*
to bomb· *bomb*
to fire· *fire*
to rob· *robber*
to mug· *mugger*
thief· theft
to fight· *fight*
to flee· *flight*

synonyms:
to flee ≈ to run away

irregular verbs:
to shoot· shot· shot
to blow (up)· blew· blown
to break· broke· broken
to steal· stole· stolen
to fight· fought· fought

irregular plurals:
a thief· two thieves

Beispielsätze: Police officers regularly stop drivers for a breathalyser test.

Pistols, guns, revolvers, rifles and knives are weapons.
Terrorists often kill innocent people by blowing up cars or buildings.

The kidnappers have threatened to use violence if they don't get 500, 000 dollars.

Law and order / Crime

gangster	Gangster/in
getaway	Flucht
harassment	Belästigung
to harm	schaden
to injure	verletzen
to insult	beleidigen
massacre	Massaker
pickpocket	Taschendieb
raid	Überfall
rebel	Rebell
conspiracy	Verschwörung
trap	Falle

trap

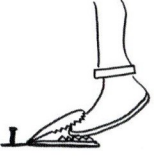

pickpocket

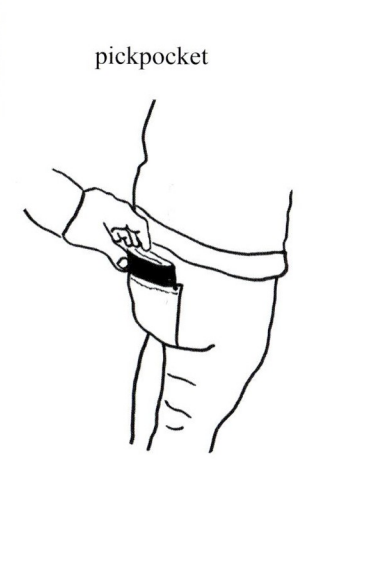

evil	böse, übel
to struggle	kämpfen
survivor	Überlebende/r
to threaten	drohen
violence	Gewalt
to wreck	zertrümmern
to crash	(zusammen-)krachen
cruel	grausam
to hide	(sich) verstecken
to horrify	entsetzen
murder	Mord
to kill	töten, umbringen
knife, knives	Messer
to lie	lügen
probable	wahrscheinlich, vermutlich
motive	Motiv

word families:
to harass · *harassment*
to injure · *injury*
rebel · rebellious
to struggle · *struggle*
to survive · *survivor* · *survival*
to threaten · *threat*
violence · violent
to wreck · *wreck*
to crash · *crash*
cruelty · cruel
to horrify · *horror* · horrible
to lie · *lie*

synonyms:
to injure ≈ to hurt
to struggle ≈ to fight
to wreck ≈ to destroy
to horrify ≈ to terrify

opposites:
evil↔good
to lie↔to tell the truth

irregular verbs:
to hide · hid · hidden

irregular plurals:
a knife · two knives

Beispielsätze:
You can't take knives with you on a plane.
The pickpocket managed to steal a purse without being noticed.
The survivors of the massacre have threatened to take revenge. That means that more violence will be used.
Murder is a terrible crime.

War and Military

army	Armee, Heer
soldier	Soldat
general	General
colonel	Oberst
to invade	eindringen, überfallen
navy	Marine
fleet	Flotte
to defend	verteidigen
to attack	angreifen
to occupy	besetzen
spy	Spion/in
sword	Schwert
troops	Truppen
victory	Sieg
to wound	verwunden
enemy	Feind/in
hero, heroes	Held, Helden
medal	Orden

World War I   1914-1918

deaths: over 17 million people

World War II   1939-1945

deaths: over 60 million people

World War I	Erster Weltkrieg
World War II	Zweiter Weltkrieg
nuclear bomb	Atombombe
peace corps	Friedenstruppen
terrorist	Terrorist
shooting	Schießerei
explosion	Explosion
peace	Frieden
shelter	Schutz
to force s.o. to do s.th.	jdn. zwingen, etwas zu tun

a symbol for peace

word families:
to invade · *invasion* · invaded
to defend · *defence*
to attack · *attack*
to occupy · *occupation* · occupied
to spy · *spy*
to wound · *wound* · wounded
to shoot · *shooting* · shot
to explode · *explosion* · explosive
to shelter · *shelter* · sheltered
to force · *force* · forced

synonyms:
to wound ≈ to injure
explosion ≈ blast
shelter ≈ protection

opposites:
to defend↔to attack
victory↔defeat
enemy↔friend
peace↔war

Beispielsätze: The main purpose of an army is to defend the nation if foreign troops attack it and try to occupy the country.
Germany invaded Poland in 1939 and started World War II.
The first nuclear bomb was dropped over Hiroshima by the US forces in August 1945.
Politicians should always try to find peaceful solutions when there are conflicts between nations.
007 is the world's most famous spy. In the movies he is portrayed as a hero who often has to rescue the world.

Religion and Ethics

religion	Religion
Christianity	Christentum
Christian	Christ/in, christlich
Protestant	Protestant/in, protestantisch
Catholic	Katholik/in, katholisch

Judaism	Judentum
Jew	Jude, Jüdin
Jewish	jüdisch

Puritan	Puritaner/in, puritanisch
Quaker	Quäker/in
Islam	Islam
Muslim	Moslem/Moslemin
Islamic	islamisch
Buddhism	Buddhismus
Buddhist	Buddhist/in, buddhistisch
Hinduism	Hinduismus
Hindu	Hindu, hinduistisch

pope	Papst
pilgrim	Pilger/in
priest	Priester/in, Pfarrer/in
bishop	Bischof
nun	Nonne
monk	Mönch

rituals	Rituale
to bless	segnen
ceremony	Zeremonie
holy	heilig
to pray	beten
procession	Umzug, Prozession
symbol	Symbol, Zeichen
funeral	Begräbnis
to baptise	taufen
sacred	heilig

word families:
Christianity · Christian
Judaism · Jewish
Buddhism · Buddhist
Hinduism · Hindu
to bless · *blessing* · blessed
to pray · *prayer*
to baptise · *baptism*

synonyms:
sacred ≈ holy

Beispielsätze: There are many religions such as Christianity, Judaism, Islam, Buddhism and Hinduism.
Every religion has its own rituals and ceremonies.
In the Christian religion, children are baptized with water.

A monastery is a place where monks live, work and pray together.

Religion and Ethics

buildings	Gebäude
church	Kirche
chapel	Kapelle
temple	Tempel
cathedral	Kathedrale
monastery	Kloster für Mönche
convent	Kloster für Nonnen
mosque	Moschee

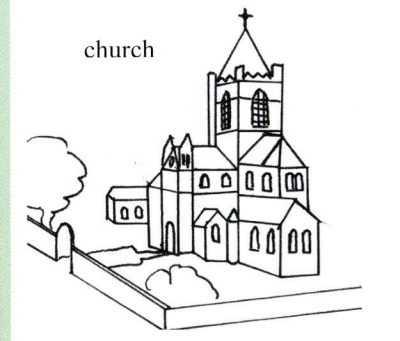

church

special days	besondere Tage
Christmas	Weihnachten
Easter	Ostern
Thanksgiving	Erntedankfest
Whitsun	Pfingsten
Ramadan	Fastenmonat für Muslime

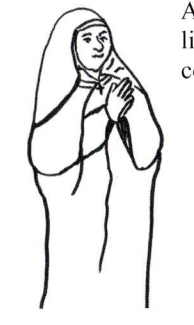 A nun usually lives in a convent.

to believe	glauben
rebirth, reincarnation	Wiedergeburt
soul	Seele
god/ goddess	Gott/ Göttin
heaven	Himmel
hell	Hölle
paradise	Paradies
sin	Sünde

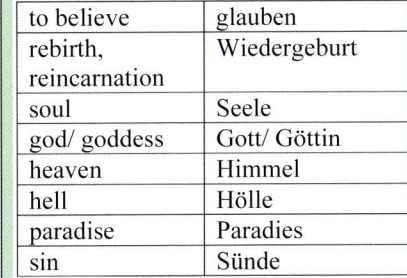 angel

word families:
to believe · *belief*

opposites:
heaven↔hell

Beispielsätze: Hindus believe in rebirth. According to their religion, the soul begins a new life in a new body after death.
Christmas and Easter are the most important celebrations for Christians.
Ramadan is the ninth month of the Islamic calendar. Muslims don't eat or drink from dawn to sunset during this time.

Culture and Entertainment

box office	Theater-, Kinokasse
ticket	Karte
circus	Zirkus
juggler	Jongleur
clown	Clown
magician	Zauberer
glamorous	glanzvoll
highlight	Höhepunkt
location	Standort, Lage
theme park	Freizeitpark
casino	Spielbank, Kasino
gambler	Zocker/in
cinema	Kino
movie/ film	Film
theatre	Theater
disco	Diskothek
disc-jockey	DJ
to dance	tanzen

exhibition	Ausstellung
gallery	Galerie
to show round	herumführen
event	Veranstaltung
festival	Festival
to organize	organisieren
to fascinate	faszinieren
marvellous	fabelhaft
spectacular	sensationell
surprising	überraschend
magnificent	herrlich, großartig
magical	zauberhaft
radio	Radio
to talk	reden, sprechen
to tell	erzählen

television	Fernsehen
production	Produktion
series	Fernsehserie/n
soap opera	Seifenoper
talk show	Talkshow
chat show	Talkshow
comedy	Komödie
comedian	Komiker
well-known	berühmt
famous	berühmt
programme	Sendung
channel	Kanal
to watch	(zu-)schauen
documentary	Dokumentation
horoscope	Horoskop
joke	Witz
puzzle	Rätsel
quiz	Quiz
cartoon	Cartoon

word families:
to juggle· *juggler*
the magic· *magician*· magic
glamour· glamorous
to highlight · *highlight*
to locate· *location*· local
to gamble· *gambler*
to dance· *dancer*
to exhibit· *exhibition*
to organize· *organization*
to fascinate· *fascination*· fascinating
to surprise· *surprise*· surprising
to talk· *talk*
to tell· *tale*
to produce· *production*
comedy· *comedian*
fame· famous
cartoon· *cartoonist*

synonyms:
marvellous ≈ brilliant
well-known ≈ famous

Beispielsätze: There is a Canadian circus here in London next month. It is a mixture of circus arts and street entertainment.
It must be marvellous with great jugglers, magicians, clowns and the world's best artists.
You can buy tickets at the box office or online.

Most people go to a casino and expect to win money there. Gambling can become a serious addiction, though. There are support groups that offer help to gamblers who want to solve their problems.

Culture and Entertainment

fair	Volksfest
raffle	Verlosung, Tombola
roller coaster	Achterbahn
dodgem car	Autoscooter
ride	Fahrt, Ritt
fun	Spaß
toy	Spielzeug
fireworks	Feuerwerk
party	Feier
karaoke	Karaoke
carnival	Karneval, Volksfest
costume	Verkleidung
to be fond of	mögen, gern haben
grand	großartig, prachtvoll

There is always a long queue at the cinema on Friday nights.

pleasant	angenehm
popular	beliebt, weitverbreitet
light	Licht
to like	mögen
to prefer	bevorzugen
to request	anfragen, verlangen
nonsense	Unsinn
queue	Schlange
to queue (B.E.)	Schlange stehen
to stand in line (A.E.)	Schlange stehen

word families:
to ride · *ride*
to have fun · *fun* · funny
to please · *pleasure* · pleasant
to popularize · *popularity* · popular
to prefer · *preference*
to request · *request* · requested
to queue · *queue*

synonyms:
fun ≈ joy
to be fond of ≈ to like
grand ≈ terrific
pleasant ≈ nice

opposites:
pleasant↔unpleasant
to like↔to dislike
popular↔unpopular

Beispielsätze: There is a fair in Nottingham in October every year with lots of different rides.

Enjoy a ride on the big wheel, the dodgem cars or the roller coaster!
There are also fireworks. Crowds of people come to enjoy the sparkling lights at night.

Arts and Music

work of art	Kunstwerk
artist	Künstler/in
mask	Maske
sketch	Sketch
music	Musik
to perform	aufführen
prize	Preis, Gewinn, Auszeichnung
audience	Publikum
listener	Zuhörer/in
to clap	klatschen
applause	Applaus
to create	schaffen
sculpture	Skulptur
statue	Standbild, Statue
carving	Schnitzerei
frame	Rahmen
painting	Gemälde, Bild
picture	Bild

song	Lied
lyrics (sg+pl)	Liedtext(e)
tune	Melodie
instrument	Instrument
bagpipes (pl)	Dudelsack
bass	Bass
drums	Schlagzeug
trumpet	Trompete
didgeridoo	Didgeridoo
guitar	Gitarre
string	Saite
piano	Klavier
saxophone	Saxofon
clarinet	Klarinette
orchestra	Orchester
choir	Chor
band	Musikgruppe, Kapelle, Band
to rehearse	proben
sound	Ton, Klang

concert	Konzert
record	Schallplatte
musical	musikalisch, Musical
opera	Oper
style	Stil
classical music	klassische Musik
folk	Folk
extraordinary	außergewöhnlich
fine	schön, fein

violin   bagpipes

word families:
art· artist
music· musical· musical
to perform· *performance*
to listen· *listener*
to create· *creation·* creative
to sculpt· to sculpture· *sculpture*
to carve· *carving*
to paint· *painting*
to sing· *song*
to drum· *drums· drummer*
guitar· guitarist
to rehearse· *rehearsal*
to sound· *sound*
to record· *recording· record*

synonyms:
fine ≈ nice

opposites:
ordinary↔extraordinary

Beispielsätze:
Rodin was a very creative artist. His sculptures are beautiful.
The National Gallery in London houses one of the finest collections of paintings in the world.
There are always interesting exhibitions at the Tate Gallery in London.
If you are interested in classical music you might want to go to a concert by the London Philharmonic Orchestra. The best way to secure tickets is to book months in advance.
Do you play an instrument? Yes, I play the piano (the guitar, the trumpet, …)

Time

day	Tag
morning	Morgen
midday	Mittag
afternoon	Nachmittag
evening	Abend
night	Nacht
midnight	Mitternacht
year	Jahr
annual	jährlich
century	Jahrhundert
seasons	Jahreszeiten
spring	Frühling
summer	Sommer
autumn (B.E.)	Herbst
fall (A.E.)	Herbst
winter	Winter

watch

months	Monate
January	Januar
February	Februar
March	März
April	April
May	Mai
June	Juni
July	Juli
August	August
September	September
October	Oktober
November	November
December	Dezember
calendar	Kalender

Daffodils blossom in spring.

days of the week	Wochentage
Monday	Montag
Tuesday	Dienstag
Wednesday	Mittwoch
Thursday	Donnerstag
Friday	Freitag
Saturday	Samstag
Sunday	Sonntag

time	Zeit
one o'clock	ein Uhr
quarter	viertel
hour	Stunde
half an hour	eine halbe Stunde
minute	Minute
second	Sekunde
clock	Uhr
watch	Armbanduhr

opposites:
day↔night
morning↔evening

prepositions:
<u>at</u> three o'clock
<u>on</u> Monday
<u>in</u> the morning
<u>in</u> July
<u>in</u> spring
<u>from</u> three <u>to</u> four o'clock
<u>between</u> three and four o'clock

Beispielsätze:
In the morning Brenda usually has breakfast at seven o'clock.
At midday she has lunch in the canteen.
In the afternoon she often goes to a café near her office.
In July she is going to travel to Scotland.
She booked her holiday on Saturday last week.
What's the time, please?
It's quarter to nine. (8.45) / It's half past three. (3.30) / It's ten minutes to seven. (6.50)

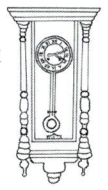

clock

Time

on time	pünktlich
in time	rechtzeitig
overnight	über Nacht
today	heute
tomorrow	morgen
yesterday	gestern
the day after tomorrow	übermorgen
the day before yesterday	vorgestern
next …	nächste(n), nächstes …
… ago	vor …
last …	letzte(n), letztes …

once	einmal
twice	zweimal
three times	dreimal
at once	sofort
during	während
soon	bald
sooner or later	früher oder später

"You have to be on time! You can't be late for the meeting!"

now	jetzt
at the moment	gerade, im Augenblick
nowadays	heutzutage
future	Zukunft
past	Vergangenheit
present	Gegenwart
recently	neulich, kürzlich
always	immer
ever	jemals
never	niemals
seldom	selten
often	oft
not … yet	noch nicht
after	nach
afterwards	danach
before	vor
hardly	kaum

opposites:
next↔last
future↔past
always↔never
often↔hardly
after↔before

prepositions:
on time
in time
at the moment

Beispielsätze: I would like to be on time for the meeting.
We have been late twice so far and Sally has not been happy about that.
She is always there first.
After the meeting we can go out for dinner. I have hardly eaten anything today.

Time

so far	bis jetzt
since	seit (Zeitpunkt)
for	seit (Zeitraum)
just	eben, gerade
already	schon
before long	in Kürze, bald
every day	jeden Tag
forever	für immer
late	spät, verspätet
later	später
meanwhile	zwischenzeitlich, inzwischen
suddenly	plötzlich
until	bis

"I have been waiting here since two o'clock."

while	während
then	dann, danach, damals
in the end	am Ende, letztlich
now and then	ab und zu
gradually	allmählich
finally	schließlich, endlich, letztendlich

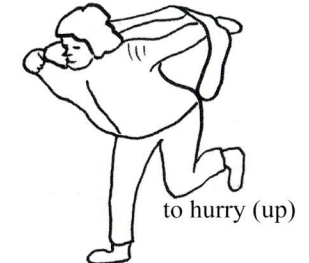

to hurry (up)

endless	endlos
immediately	sofort, unverzüglich
occasionally	gelegentlich
ultimately	schlussendlich, letztendlich
to hurry (up)	sich beeilen
to last	dauern
to start	beginnen, anfangen
to stop	aufhören, anhalten
to wait	warten
early	früh

synonyms:
immediately ≈ at once
occasionally ≈ sometimes
to start ≈ to begin

opposites:
late↔early
to start↔to stop

prepositions:
for three weeks (Zeitraum)
since Monday (Zeitpunkt)
in the end

Beispielsätze:

Mike has just gone to the living room to make a phone call.
He has been waiting for a mechanic for half an hour.

Brenda and Lucy have known each other since they were children.
They had been neighbours until Lucy's parents moved house.

Measures / Quantities / Comparisons

weight	Gewicht
gram	Gramm
ounce	Unze (28,35g)
pound	Pfund (lb) = 454 g
kilogram	Kilogramm
ton	Tonne
scales	Waage

length	Länge
centimetre	Zentimeter
metre	Meter
kilometre	Kilometer
inch	Zoll (2,54 cm)
foot	1 Fuß =12 Zoll (30,48 cm)
yard	1 yard = 3 Fuß = 0.914m
mile	1,609 km

a bit	ein bisschen
a few	einige
a lot of	viele
about	ungefähr
almost	fast, beinahe
half	halb
lots of	viele
many	viele
much	viel
several	einige
amount	Menge
another	ein weiterer, ein anderer
low	niedrig, tief, gering
near	nahe, in der Nähe von
far	weit, fern
small	klein
empty	leer

to weigh	wiegen
heavy	schwer
high	hoch
huge	riesig
large	groß
little, small	klein
tremendous	enorm, gewaltig
tiny	winzig
short	kurz
long	lang
narrow	schmal, eng
full	voll
total	völlig, gesamt
giant, gigantic	riesig
to carry	tragen
to lift	heben
quick	schnell
slow	langsam
fast	schnell
rapid	rasch, schnell

synonyms:

several ≈ some
huge ≈ giant ≈ gigantic
quick ≈ fast ≈ rapid

opposites:

a bit↔a lot
a lot of↔a few
many↔a few
much↔little
low↔high
near↔far
small↔big, large
empty↔full
heavy↔light
huge, gigantic↔tiny
short↔long
narrow↔wide
quick, fast↔slow

Beispielsätze:
Mandy's house is as big as a castle.
It was not as expensive as I had thought.
It was cheaper than ours.
Look at these huge skyscrapers! When you are at the top of such a gigantic building, everything seems so tiny when you look down.

Colours

green	grün
red	rot
blue	blau
yellow	gelb
white	weiß
orange	orange
brown	braun
grey	grau
pink	rosa, pink
turquoise	türkis
purple	lila
violet	violett
black	schwarz
dark	dunkel
light	hell
colourful	farbenfroh
multi-coloured	mehrfarbig

Paint the fields with different colours.

Beispielsätze: Some people are red-green colour blind.

Most little girls love anything that is pink.

Verbs with Prepositions / Phrasal verbs

to agree with	übereinstimmen mit
to aim at	(ab-) zielen auf
to answer to	antworten auf
to apologize for	sich entschuldigen für
to approve of	gutheißen, zustimmen zu
to ask for	bitten um, fragen nach
to be afraid of	Angst haben vor
to be away	weg sein
to be down	niedergeschlagen sein
to be fond of	mögen
to be in	da sein, zuhause sein
to belong to	gehören
to boil over	überkochen
to break down	zusammenbrechen, kaputt gehen

to break in	einbrechen
to break off	abbrechen
to break out	ausbrechen
to break through	durchbrechen
to breathe out	ausatmen
to bring along	mitbringen
to bring back	zurückbringen
to brush up	verbessern
to build up	aufbauen
to bump into	zufällig treffen, anrempeln, aufeinander treffen
to burst into	ausbrechen in (z.B. Lachen)
to calm down	sich beruhigen, ruhig werden
to carry on	weitermachen
to cheer up	aufheitern
to come from	kommen aus

to complain about	sich beschweren über
to count on	zählen auf
to concentrate on	sich konzentrieren auf
to consist of	bestehen aus
to cope with	fertig werden mit, bewältigen
to cut back on	reduzieren
to cut down	kürzen, einschränken, einsparen
to cut off	unterbrechen
to deal with	behandeln, zum Thema haben, sich befassen mit

word families:
to agree · *agreement*
to aim · *aim*
to answer · *answer*
to apologize · *apology*
to approve · *approval*
to complain · *complaint*
to concentrate · *concentration*

synonyms:
to carry on ≈ to go on, to continue
to cut back on ≈ to reduce

opposites:
to break off ↔ to start
to breathe out ↔ to breathe in
to calm down ↔ to get excited
to carry on ↔ to stop

Beispielsätze:
Sally was late because she had bumped into her ex-boyfriend in town.
He broke off the relationship last year.
Sally was very excited after meeting him and we told her to calm down a bit.
She apologized for keeping us waiting.
Of course, we could understand that she wanted to talk to him.

Verbs with Prepositions / Phrasal verbs

to depend on	abhängen von	to get on	einsteigen, miteinander aus-kommen	to hand out	austeilen
to dream of / about	träumen von			to hand over	überreichen
to die out	aussterben	to get out	herauskommen	to hang around	herumhängen
to disagree with	nicht zustimmen zu, nicht über-einstimmen mit	to get over	bewältigen, über-winden	to hold back	zurückhalten
				to hold on	festhalten
		to get to	ankommen, erreichen	Hold on!	Warte! (Auffor-derung)
to end up	enden, landen				
to escape from	entkommen von, fliehen vor	to get together	zusammenkommen	to hurry up	sich beeilen
		to get up	aufstehen	to identify with	sich identifizieren mit
to find out	herausfinden	to give back	zurückgeben		
to get away	entkommen, wegkommen	to give up	aufgeben		
		to go ahead	weitermachen	to insist on	bestehen auf
to get back	zurückkommen	to go away	weggehen	to keep on	weitermachen
to get by	auskommen	to go off	schlecht werden (Lebensmittel)	to keep up	fortfahren, aufrechterhalten
to get in	hineinkommen				
to get off	aussteigen	to go on	weitermachen	to knock down	niederschlagen
		to go out	ausgehen	to knock out	außer Gefecht setzen, k.o. schlagen
		to go through	durchgehen		
		to grow up	aufwachsen		
		to hand in	einreichen	to laugh at	lachen über

word families:
to depend · *dependence*
to dream · *dream*
to end · *end*
to escape · *escape*
to identify · *identification*
to laugh · *laughter*

synonyms:
to get back ≈ to return
to get together ≈ to meet
to give back ≈ to return
to go ahead ≈ to go on

opposites:
to get back ↔ to leave
to get in ↔ to get out
to get up ↔ to go to bed
to go ahead ↔ to stop
to keep on ↔ to stop
to hand in ↔ to hand out

Beispielsätze: Harry dreams about becoming a pilot.
It all depends on the tests he has to do.
We will soon find out if he has passed.
He will be back tomorrow.
It would be hard for him to give up his dream if he didn't pass.

71

Verbs with Prepositions / Phrasal verbs

to lay down	hinlegen (etwas)
to lie down	sich hinlegen
to light up	erleuchten
to look after	sich kümmern um
to look around	umschauen
to look at	anschauen
to look back	zurückschauen
to look for	suchen
to look forward to	sich freuen auf
to look up	nachschauen, nachschlagen
to make up your mind	sich entscheiden
to make up	sich ausdenken
to meet with	sich treffen mit
to pay back	zurückzahlen
to pay for	bezahlen für
to pick out	auswählen
to play with	spielen mit
to plug in	einstecken (Stecker)

to point out	hervorheben
to put off	aufschieben
to settle down	sich niederlassen
to sit down	sich hinsetzen
to slow down	langsamer werden
to speak up	lauter sprechen
to speed up	schneller werden
to split up	sich trennen
to succeed in	Erfolg haben mit
to switch off	ausschalten (Gerät)
to switch on	einschalten (Gerät)
to take apart	auseinanderlegen
to take away	wegnehmen
to take back	zurücknehmen
to take off	abheben (Flugzeug), losfahren, ausziehen (Kleidung)

to take over	übernehmen
to tidy up	aufräumen
to try on	anprobieren
to try out	ausprobieren
to turn away	wegdrehen, ablehnen
to turn back	umkehren, zurückdrehen
to turn down	ablehnen, zurückweisen
to turn into	werden .. zu
to turn off	ausschalten (Gerät)
to turn on	einschalten (Gerät)
to turn out	sich herausstellen
to turn up	auftauchen
to wake up	aufwachen
to watch out for	sich in Acht nehmen vor, aufpassen bei

word families:
to light · *light*
to settle · *settlement*
to speed · *speed*
to succeed · *success* · successful
to switch · *switch*

synonyms:
to look for ≈ to search
to make up your mind ≈ to decide
to pick out ≈ to choose
to put off ≈ to delay
to switch on ≈ to turn on
to switch off ≈ to turn off

opposites:
to lay down↔to pick up
to lie down↔to get up
to look after↔to neglect
to look for↔to find
to sit down↔to get up, to stand up
to slow down↔to speed up
to succeed in↔to fail
to take off↔to land
to turn down↔to accept

Beispielsätze:
Mike is looking forward to going to university in the States.
He has made up his mind to study law in New York.
It is quite expensive because he has to pay for tuition.
The rent has also turned out to be higher than he thought.
Luckily, his parents support him financially.
He hopes that one day he will be able to pay some of the money back to them.

Nouns and Adjectives with Prepositions

advantage of	Vorteil von
attitude to / towards	Einstellung zu
chance of	Chance zu
difficulty in	Schwierigkeit bei
doubt about	Zweifel über
experience in	Erfahrung mit
impression on	Eindruck auf
interest in	Interesse an
increase in	Anstieg an
opportunity to	Gelegenheit zu
place for	Platz zum / für
possibility of	Möglichkeit zu
reason for	Grund für
solution to	Lösung für
way of	Art und Weise zu

angry about/ with	verärgert über, böse, verärgert mit
bored with	gelangweilt von
capable of	fähig zu
dependent on	abhängig von
different from	unterschiedlich zu
famous for	berühmt für
glad about	froh über
good at	gut in
impressed by	beeindruckt von
interested in	interessiert an
keen on	begeistert von

proud of	stolz auf
tired of	genug haben von
worried about	besorgt über

word families:
to doubt · *doubt*
to impress · *impression* · impressed
to interest · *interest* · interesting
to increase · *increase*
to solve · *solution*
anger · angry
boredom · bored
to depend · *dependence* · dependent
to differ · *difference* · different
fame · famous
gladness · glad
pride · proud
tiredness · tired
to worry · *worry* · worried

synonyms:
chance of ≈ opportunity to

opposites:
advantage↔disadvantage
increase↔decrease
bored↔interested
dependent↔independent
good↔bad

Beispielsätze:
There is still a chance of winning the championship.
There is no reason for giving up now.
The coach will definitely find a solution to the problem the team has with the injuries of three defenders.
You shouldn't forget that there are a number of players who are good at scoring goals.
They are capable of surprising the opponent.

Irregular Verbs

Infinitive	Simple Past	Past Participle	German
to be	was	been	sein
to beat	beat	beaten	schlagen
to become	became	become	werden
to begin	began	begun	beginnen
to bite	bit	bitten	beißen
to bend	bent	bent	verbiegen
to blow	blew	blown	blasen
to break	broke	broken	brechen
to bring	brought	brought	bringen
to build	built	built	bauen
to burn	burnt	burnt	brennen

Infinitive	Simple Past	Past Participle	German
to buy	bought	bought	kaufen
to catch	caught	caught	fangen
to choose	chose	chosen	wählen, aussuchen
to come	came	come	kommen
to cost	cost	cost	kosten
to cut	cut	cut	schneiden
to deal	dealt	dealt	handeln
to dig	dug	dug	graben
to do	did	done	machen, tun
to draw	drew	drawn	zeichnen
to dream	dreamt / dreamed	dreamt / dreamed	träumen

Infinitive	Simple Past	Past Participle	German
to drink	drank	drunk	trinken
to drive	drove	driven	fahren
to eat	ate	eaten	essen
to fall	fell	fallen	fallen
to feed	fed	fed	füttern
to feel	felt	felt	fühlen
to fight	fought	fought	kämpfen
to find	found	found	finden
to flee	fled	fled	fliehen, flüchten
to fly	flew	flown	fliegen
to forget	forgot	forgotten	vergessen

Infinitive	Simple Past	Past Participle	German
to freeze	froze	frozen	(ge)frieren
to get	got	got	holen, bekommen
to give	gave	given	geben
to go	went	gone	gehen, fahren
to grow	grew	grown	(an)pflanzen, wachsen
to hang	hung	hung	hängen
to have	had	had	haben
to hear	heard	heard	hören
to hide	hid	hidden	verbergen, verstecken
to hit	hit	hit	treffen, schlagen
to hold	held	held	halten

Infinitive	Simple Past	Past Participle	German
to hurt	hurt	hurt	verletzen, schmerzen
to keep	kept	kept	halten, behalten
to know	knew	known	wissen, kennen
to lay	laid	laid	legen, setzen, stellen
to lead	led	led	führen, leiten
to lean	leant	leant	sich lehnen
to learn	learnt / learned	learnt / learned	lernen, erfahren
to leave	left	left	verlassen
to lend	lent	lent	verleihen, ausborgen
to let	let	let	lassen, zulassen
to lie	lay	lain	liegen

Infinitive	Simple Past	Past Participle	German
to light	lit	lit	anzünden
to lose	lost	lost	verlieren
to make	made	made	machen
to mean	meant	meant	bedeuten, meinen
to meet	met	met	treffen, begegnen
to overtake	overtook	overtaken	überholen
to pay	paid	paid	bezahlen
to put	put	put	setzen, stellen
to read	read	read	lesen
to ride	rode	ridden	reiten
to rise	rose	risen	aufgehen, aufsteigen

Infinitive	Simple Past	Past Participle	German
to ring	rang	rung	klingeln, anrufen
to run	ran	run	laufen
to say	said	said	sagen
to see	saw	seen	sehen
to sell	sold	sold	verkaufen
to send	sent	sent	schicken, senden
to set	set	set	festlegen, festsetzen, stellen
to shake	shook	shaken	schütteln
to shine	shone	shone	scheinen, polieren
to shoot	shot	shot	schießen

Infinitive	Simple Past	Past Participle	German
to show	showed	shown / showed	zeigen
to shut	shut	shut	schließen
to sing	sang	sung	singen
to sink	sank	sunk	sinken
to sit	sat	sat	sitzen
to sleep	slept	slept	schlafen
to slide	slid	slid	gleiten, rutschen
to smell	smelt	smelt	riechen
to speak	spoke	spoken	sprechen
to spend	spent	spent	verbringen, ausgeben

Infinitive	Simple Past	Past Participle	German
to spill	spilt / spilled	spilt / spilled	verschütten, vergießen
to spin	span / spun	spun	drehen, spinnen
to spit	spat	spat	spucken
to spoil	spoilt / spoiled	spoilt / spoiled	verderben
to spread	spread	spread	verbreiten
to stand	stood	stood	stehen
to steal	stole	stolen	stehlen
to swear	swore	sworn	schwören, fluchen
to sweep	swept	swept	fegen, kehren
to swim	swam	swum	schwimmen
to take	took	taken	nehmen

Infinitive	Simple Past	Past Participle	German
to teach	taught	taught	unterrichten, lehren
to tear	tore	torn	zerreißen
to tell	told	told	erzählen
to think	thought	thought	denken, glauben
to throw	threw	thrown	werfen
to understand	understood	understood	verstehen
to wake	woke	woken	wecken, aufwachen
to wear	wore	worn	tragen
to win	won	won	gewinnen
to write	wrote	written	schreiben